SpringerBriefs in Computer Science

Series Editors

Stan Zdonik
Peng Ning
Shashi Shekhar
Jonathan Katz
Xindong Wu
Lakhmi C. Jain
David Padua
Xuemin Shen
Borko Furht
V. S. Subrahmanian
Martial Hebert
Katsushi Ikeuchi
Bruno Siciliano

For further volumes:
http://www.springer.com/series/10028

SpringerBriefs in Computer Science

Ali al-Azzawi

Experience with Technology

Dynamics of User Experience
with Mobile Media Devices

Springer

Ali al-Azzawi
Digital World Research Centre
University of Surrey
Guildford, Surrey
UK

ISSN 2191-5768   ISSN 2191-5776   (electronic)
ISBN 978-1-4471-5396-2   ISBN 978-1-4471-5397-9   (eBook)
DOI 10.1007/978-1-4471-5397-9
Springer London Heidelberg New York Dordrecht

Library of Congress Control Number: 2013944515

Printed on acid-free paper

Springer is part of Springer Science+Business Media (www.springer.com)

For Mama, Baba, Rachel and my daughters,
Hannah, Amaani, Leila and Mariam

Foreword

Experience with Technology reports the Ph.D. work of Ali al-Azzawi while based at Digital World Research Centre and the Department of Psychology, University of Surrey. This context is important to the intellectual orientation of the enquiry, since Digital World is focussed on the design of new media systems while the Department of Psychology is concerned with the fundamental understanding of internal psychological processes. Bringing together these perspectives, through Ali's creativity and enthusiasm was an exciting process for us all and the results, reported in this book, are a novel and theoretically grounded insight into the way people make sense of everyday technology.

Within this context, Ali chose to examine the psychology of experience with digital media technology and its relation to various design attributes of MP3 music players of the Ph.D. period (2005–2010). His findings are therefore relevant both to the design of digital media devices and to the relationships we have with many similar 'gadgets' in our lives, especially as they unfold and deepen over time and use. In fact, the dynamic and changing nature of those relationships and their sensitivity to different layers of design turns out to be one of the main discoveries and insights of the work.

The theoretical lens chosen to examine experience with technology is that of the personal construct. This notion was introduced by George Kelly in his 1955 book entitled 'The psychology of personal constructs'. According to Kelly, personal constructs are the concepts we use to categorise things in the world and make sense of our experience with them. He illustrates and embodies this insight in a simple 'repertory grid' technique of asking people to sort three objects into two groups showing what is the same and different about them. If you try this now for any three objects in your field of view, you will find that the criterion you use to do this sorting is important to the way you think about the objects, and quite specific to you personally. In this book, Ali uses a variation of the repertory grid technique to get people sorting different kinds of MP3 players, at different stages of use. By talking to them about the criteria they use and analysing patterns of sorting across groups of participants, it is possible to expose a secret world of perceptions (constructs) not available by interview alone. Surprisingly, this has seldom been applied to interactive products before, and never with a view to developing personal construct theory in this domain. Ali does both these things to reveal a variety of new findings regarding the perception of digital devices, as well as developing a new model of user experience based on the evolution of personal constructs over time.

Three studies reported in the book unfold to provide a unique insight into people's experiences with technology and potentially with the other objects we choose to interact with. In the first study, a structured sorting task provides access to the constructs people employ to make initial judgements about MP3 players and the way they shape their views of 'beauty'. These constructs are then used to produce a new questionnaire for measuring user experience. In the second study, this questionnaire is used by 16 participants to rate four canonical MP3 designs, before and after interaction with them. The findings reveal a number of 'super constructs' describing users' changing experience with the devices, including novelty, usability, complexity, aesthetics and physicality. A concise set of constructs are provided in the form of a UX-Scale in Appendix D, and can now be freely used to create a UX profile for any interactive product, based on these super constructs. The third study goes on to provide innovative links between theories of cycles of consumption and those of changing experience over time, and turn to examine how people's relationships with and expectations of technology change from purchase through use to replacement. Following eight users through real time, the final study provides an insight into their thoughts and feelings around the devices they actually bought. In the closing chapters, the book brings together the various streams of theory and empirical results to form an integrative theory of experience.

The book integrates diverse literatures on user experience and presents new findings and concepts. It should therefore be of value to both academics and researchers seeking to understand the area in greater depth and to practitioners seeking to shape our experience with new products and services in a more customised and personal way.

University of Surrey, June 2013   Prof. David Frohlich
                                                                                      Dr. Margaret Wilson

Endorsement

Experience with Technology provides some missing DNA to the world of HCI. I am impressed with how Dr. al-Azzawi brings in literatures that are often neglected by mainline user researchers, e.g. social theory, categorization, and brand. He does so in a thoughtful and compelling manner. The scholarship is thorough and top-notch, especially in the synthesis of it all in his ICE model. This book straddles the line that is often hard to manage; it serves as a solid foundation for academic coursework as well as an impetus for practical application of theory. In it all, his writing is lucid and pithy; there is not a wasted word. I strongly recommend this to HCI practitioners who believe there is nothing new in the field. There is, and it is within the pages of this book.

Robert Schumacher

Preface

While working as a physicist and an engineer, installing, supporting and servicing MRI scanners around the world, I became acutely aware of how some machines, in comparison with others, seemed easier to run, maintain and fix. The difference appeared to be linked to features such as the small LEDs that indicate whether a hardware module is on, off, or on standby. Such basic aspects of the implied user interface seemed to have escaped the attention of the designers of these high quality machines, manufactured to high technical standards. Somehow, it felt as though they had not always considered the user, even another technical user. These kinds of frustrations were the seeds that led eventually to my desire to investigate how people experience technology and to learn more about ways to improve the user experience. So, after many years of running a web development company, I eventually embarked on a research project at the University of Surrey which I envisaged would help me to better understand how people experience technology, with the hope also that the project would contribute to the vast body of knowledge across the fields of design, psychology, and Human-Computer Interaction (HCI).

This book brings together a summary of some of the key ideas, thoughts and approaches from within the HCI, design, marketing and psychology literature, as well as the main insights from my research at Surrey. These findings were made possible with the help of nearly 250 participants and with the support of many academics and fellow researchers at the Digital World Research Centre and the School of Psychology to whom I am very grateful. I am also indebted to my academic supervisors, mentors and cheerleaders, Professor David Frohlich and Dr. Margaret Wilson, whose patience and positive attitude towards their craft has truly been a great inspiration.

During this project, I found myself in the unique position of being able to draw on a range of experiences, including my early technical training and many years of involvement in design, development and business, which, in combination with my research findings, have allowed me to formulate concurrent views on the three main elements of user experience (UX): *technology*, *business* and *users*. Though still involved in academia, I have therefore returned to industry as a UX researcher and designer with the intention of making a positive, practical, and insightful contribution to this expanding commercial field. Consequently, I have attempted to keep this book focused on these main elements, remaining grounded in the realities of industry, whilst still maintaining an academic interest. The book is therefore aimed at both academic researchers and industrial practitioners alike, who are interested in exploring the theoretical understandings of how people experience technology in ways that offer an alignment of theory with practical methods. I hope you find it both useful and enjoyable.

Dubai, May 2013   Dr. Ali al-Azzawi

Contents

Chapter 1
Introduction

Abstract Opening with a recent, real-life example of the way in which the unveiling of technological artefact delighted and enchanted a captivated audience, this chapter provides an overview of the structure of the book and the rationale being adopted, highlighting the key questions being posed. The book is divided into three parts. First, a variety of theories of meaning, experience and user experience are described and contrasted, in order to provide a back-drop to the UX debate. Foundations are also laid in order to create a sense of clarity around primary terms such as *technology*, *experience*, and *meaning*. Different ways of understanding UX are then critiqued, followed by a proposal of a model of UX which I define as the ICE model (*Interaction*, *Construction*, and *Evaluation*). As well as having a sound theoretical basis, this model is derived from extensive and rigorously conducted experimental studies. The second part of the book then highlights a collection of case-studies that provide empirical support for the proposed model in terms of ways of thinking about the user experience. Finally, the third part of the book consolidates the data and findings from the case-studies and draws on additional literature in order to enrich the model with finer detail. The book concludes by proposing a number of responses to the research questions posed at the outset.

Keywords Human–computer interaction (HCI) • Mobile device usability • User experience (UX) • User experience dynamics • Personal Construct Theory (PCT) • ICE model

In January 2007, Apple Inc. launched their new iPhone to a standing ovation. The event was the MacWorld conference and their CEO, Steve Jobs, had just unveiled the design of a sleek phone that sported a touch screen interface for making phone calls, browsing the Internet, playing music and video, and taking photographs. No-one in the audience had even seen the device, let alone used it. Yet an expectation filled the auditorium that here was something special, extraordinary and above all desirable. Interestingly, even though, none of the technical functionalities were new, the response to this 'unveiling' was close to hysteria.

A. al-Azzawi, *Experience with Technology*, SpringerBriefs in Computer Science,   1
DOI: 10.1007/978-1-4471-5397-9_1, © The Author(s) 2014

The above example shows a vignette of people's experience with technology, which is the main interest in this book, although UX and consumption of mobile media devices are used as a focus within this research. Therefore, the intention is to explore the wider question of how people experience technology in general. In this broader context, UX, i.e. the actual use and physical interaction with technological artifacts, is seen as an example of the kinds of experiences that people have with technology. The same is true for consumption of such devices. Consumption is seen here as a wider view of UX, where a more encompassing and on-going narrative is taken into account, that acknowledges earlier experiences, as well as anticipated ones that are yet to occur.

Therefore, throughout this book, the reader is reminded to keep in mind this broader scope of the use of the word 'experience', and a 'user' is one who is not only having actualised physical interactions with technology, but may also having intended interactions.

According to HCI, psychology, product design and consumer literature, expectations and demands of consumers have undergone gradual changes. Where the emphasis used to be on utility and efficiency (Norman 1990), shifting to value and quality of service, and recently to products and services that provide pleasurable experiences (Jordan 1999). These changes have highlighted the need for better understanding of how people experience technology, in order to help product and service designers to create compelling user experiences (Pine and Gilmore 1999). User Experience (UX) has been defined in terms of "quality of experience ... (encompassing) all the aspects of how people use an interactive product ... way it feels ... understand how it works ... serves their purposes ... fits into the entire context" (Alben 1996, p. 12). Others have focused on the "essential characteristics of experience. Characteristics that differentiate from behaviour, practice, knowledge and other more familiar psychological categories" (Wright et al. 2003, p. 52). While, some have described it in terms of a "consequence (of three) facets ... user's internal state ... the characteristics of the designed system ... the context (or the environment)" (Hassenzahl and Tractinsky 2006, p. 95). These definitions and points of view of UX, can be useful in some respects, however, what they do not provide is a way of reconciling the tension between the seemingly reductive approaches (Hassenzahl 2004), with the holistic ones (McCarthy and Wright 2004). The reductive approaches usually present a set of Cartesian components that are seen as the building blocks of UX, without acknowledging the complex and holistic view.

This book tries to find a way of understanding UX while holding both of the above approaches, by exploring the way people come to make judgments about what kind of user experience they can expect from a new technology, from its appearance alone. A following question is about how this changes as a person approaches and then interacts with the technology. This chapter provides an introduction in order to orient the reader and make these goals clear, and to show the binding threads of this new approach.

The aim of this book is therefore to explore the notion of User Experience by combining systematic quantitative methodology and analytical techniques, with structured qualitative methods in order to maintain the richness and complexity of the data. Kelly's (1955) Personal Construct Theory (PCT) and associated methods will form some of the basis of this project, but will not be the exclusive approach. This project has three primary objectives:

1. Explore the structure of the underlying conceptualisations of technology.
2. Characterise the dynamics of user experience.
3. Use the above aims to develop a model of User Experience.

The dynamics are of interest from the point of view of short-term changes, as well as long term. Of specific interest is the role that interaction plays in shaping people's experience of technology. This project is anchored in mobile media devices, specifically MP3 players, as an exemplar of technology. However, the intention is that findings within this book are useful for informing other areas of technology use, and understanding people's interaction with them.

1.1 Theories and Studies of User Experience

The essence of this book begins in Chap. 2 by addressing the concept of 'User Experience', in order to define the terms within it. The different ways of understanding 'experience' are explored, for example, Dewey's (1934) definitions of 'experience' and 'an experience'. This exploration then moves on to the notion of time, and how people experience time, where time is sometimes an instantaneous feeling, or a retrospective one. However, such retrospective experiences are also close to Kelly's (1955) construing of events, which he proposes as part of his Personal Construct Theory. However, Kelly's proposal is a rich one that makes a full description of how people make meaning of their world, where they do this by using 'constructs'. Although the idea of constructs is not particularly new, Kelly makes a clear definition of them, which allows him to develop a clear methodological approach, within the phenomenological tradition.

Chapter 2 also explores specific proposals about the nature of UX from the HCI and psychology literature. These proposals are broadly categorised into three approaches: The first describes UX as a list of *qualities*, for example, the appearance of the product, or how it serves the user's purpose. The second category describes UX as a *consequence*, for example the arousal or pleasure that is derived from the use of an artifact. The last category is where UX is described as a collection of *processes*. For example, users engaging in reflection upon interaction with technology (McCarthy and Wright 2004; Norman 2003). Chapter 2 is then used to focus on the sense-making processes proposed by McCarthy and Wright, and to find the common aspects of these processes with Kelly's PCT, such as anticipation (Al-Azzawi et al. 2010a). This analysis then feeds into sense-making in broader terms, and the construing processes involved in understanding narratives, and relationships. The chapter ends by proposing a model of user experience where the process of *Construction* takes a role along with *Interaction* and *Evaluation* (ICE). This, model is then used to focus and guide the rest of the book.

Chapter 3 presents a critique of studies used to explore particularly construc-tive aspects of UX, such as the meaning and value in things (Csikszentmihalyi and Rochberg-Halton 1981; Richins 1994), as well as meaningful relationships, including ones where self-identity is constructed (Dittmar 1992). Other studies are then described that explore the evaluative aspects of UX, such as novelty, as well as judgement of 'goodness', where habituation effects are exhibited. Also, com-plexity and coherence are explored from an environmental psychology point of view (Kaplan and Kaplan 1989), where parallels are suggested with technology.

One aspect of UX that is explored in detail is that of aesthetics, where several previous studies have suggested that usability is closely linked to the aesthetic presentation of an artifact. Specifically of interest, are the changes in people's evaluations and the way they experience technology over time, in other words the dynamics of user experience.

The chapter also examines the different methods used to explore and measure UX, such as *experience sampling*, *content analysis*, and *grounded theory*. The focus is also brought onto methods that have a phenomenological basis and are grounded in Kelly's PCT, such *Repertory Grid Test* (RGT), and *Multiple Sorting Procedure* (MSP), in order to align the choice of methods with the underlying the-oretical basis of this research.

1.2 Empirical Studies

Chapter 4 describes the first case-study of the project, which was designed to elicit the basic constructs that people use to conceptualise mobile media devices, in this case, MP3 players (Al-Azzawi et al. 2007). The study identifies the under-lying structure of how people understand aesthetics in the context of technologi-cal artifacts, as well as the structure behind their preferences. These findings are augmented with qualitative insights into user experiences of the participants, and qualitative comparisons are made between first impressions and aesthetics of MP3 players. Another study is also described in this chapter, where the focus is on reducing the large number of constructs into dimensions of User Experience.

In relation to 'dynamics' and the notion of 'time' discussed earlier, Chap. 5 is then concerned with defining a 'frame' for experience, and the cycle of consump-tion is proposed as a useful starting point as an example of an experience cycle. For this, the Consumer Decision Process (CDP) is proposed as the basic frame-work to derive a cycle that is more customised to the consumption of technology and is therefore more suited to this current research (Blackwell et al. 2006), and is then used to provide access to long-term experience cycles.

The initial case-studies mostly identify quantitatively measurable aspects of UX, and to compliment these data, a purely qualitative exploration is also pre-sented. This section explores a case study of eight participants in a large longitu-dinal study of users going through their experiences of purchasing MP3 players, in the context of their lives, rather than a 'laboratory' setting, as well as looking closer at one of the eight individual participants. The study is based on a collection of in-depth semi-structured interviews, which are designed around the consumption cycle, tracking the individual participants *before*, *just after*, and *some time after* their acquisition of their device. The qualitative interview data are then analysed for themes and constructs that are not visible in the previously described studies, in order to build a more complete picture of users' experiences of mobile media devices. The data yielded more constructs, than detected in the initial case-studies, and in particular shed more light on the importance of relationships, in ways that were not clear from the initial studies. Relationships are found between participants and object, and with others, and the issue of brand is particularly highlighted. The data also highlight the notion of 'implications', discussed later in the book (Al-Azzawi 2012). This emphasises the idea that experience can be described as an interaction of personal, physical and social contexts.

1.3   ICE: A Proposed Model of User Experience

The final part of the book brings the discussions and data together, in relation to the proposed ICE model as a way of defining UX. ICE is then extended in the light of the empirical findings of the research. First the constructive aspects are presented, within the frame of dimensions of UX. Then the dynamic aspect of UX and how it relates to the construction processes, and the way the relationships between constructs change as interaction and consumption take place. The reader is then reminded of the issue of construct stability, as a way of classifying constructs, where evaluation and affect play a part in the way participants experience technology (Al-Azzawi et al. 2010b). Also, relationships are brought into focus in the next chapter, where the different types of relationships are discussed, and how they are used to define the 'self'. This includes, but is not exclusive to, the relationship to 'brand', where brand may be seen as a proxy and a sign for many aspects of experience. Also, types of relationships with objects are the subject of discussion, in the context of the variety of ways that 'love' can be defined. Finally, the relationship of experiences themselves, as 'experience networks', where *implications* create the richness of a psychological event. This network of experiences is then discussed as a major contributor to the holocentric basis to the ICE model.

The last chapter is then used to explore the practical implications of the findings, and show how HCI and design can take a view regarding the importance of idiosyncratic experiences that form part of UX. Also, the implications for psychology theory are discussed, where the complex and interrelated networks of experiences and constructs make it difficult to see how an exclusively reductive view of UX can be useful. The next part of the chapter takes a meta-view, questioning some of the aspects of the methodological approaches, as well as the validity of the findings. The findings are also related to other existing literature, and further research is proposed, along with new questions that have been raised by this book. Finally, a concise statement is made regarding the conclusions that may be drawn from data and discussions within the book, highlighting what are seen as the major contributions from this book, to the theory and practice regarding the fields of HCI and User Experience.

References

Al-Azzawi, A. (2012). Contradictions and implications: Making sense of apparently irrational behavior. *User Experience, 11*, 4–5.

Al-Azzawi, A., Frohlich, D., & Wilson, M. (2007). Beauty constructs for MP3 players. *CoDesign—International Journal of CoCreation in Design and the Arts, Affective Communication in Design—Challenges for Researchers* (3-S1), 59–74.

Al-Azzawi, A., Frohlich, D., & Wilson, M. (2010a). Eliciting users' experience with technology. In D. Bourne & M. Fromm (Eds.), *Construing PCP: New Contexts and Perspectives: 9th EPCA Conference Proceedings* (pp. 265–282). London: Books on Demand.

Al-Azzawi, A., Frohlich, D., & Wilson, M. (2010b). *Stability of user experience: Changes in constructs as users transition from anticipated to actualised interaction.* Paper presented at the iHCI 2010, Dublin.

Alben, L. (1996). Quality of experience: Defining the criteria for effective interaction design. *Interactions, 3*(3), 11–15.

Blackwell, R. D., Miniard, P. W., & Engel, J. F. (2006). *Consumer behaviour: International student edition* (Vol. 10). Mason OH: Thompson.

Csikszentmihalyi, M., & Rochberg-Halton, E. (1981). *The meaning of things.* Cambridge: Cambridge University Press.

Dewey, J. (1934). *Art as experience* (paperback 2005 ed.). Perigee.

Dittmar, H. (1992). *The social psychology of material possessions: To have is to be.* New York: St. Martin's Press.

Hassenzahl, M. (2004). The interplay of beauty, goodness, and usability in interactive products. *Human-Computer Interactions, 19*, 319–349.

Hassenzahl, M., & Tractinsky, N. (2006). User experience—A research agenda. *Behaviour & Information Technology, 25*(2), 91–97.

Jordan, P. W. (1999). *Designing pleasurable products: An introduction to the new human factors.* London: Taylor & Francis.

Kaplan, R., & Kaplan, S. (1989). *The experience of nature: A psychological perspective.* New York: Cambridge University Press.

Kelly, G. A. (1955). *The psychology of personal constructs, volume one: Theory and personality* (1991 ed., Vol. 1). London: Routledge.

McCarthy, J., & Wright, P. C. (2004). *Technology as experience.* Cambridge: MIT Press.

Norman, D. A. (1990). *The design of everyday things.* New York: Basic Books.

Norman, D. A. (2003). *Emotional design: Why we love (or hate) everyday things.* New York: Basic Books.

Pine, J. B., & Gilmore, J. H. (1999). *The experience economy.* Boston: Harvard Business School Press.

Richins, M. L. (1994). Valuing things: The public and private meanings of possessions. *Journal of Consumer Research, 21*(3), 504–521.

Wright, P. C., McCarthy, J., & Meekison, L. (2003). Making sense of experience. In M. A. Blyth, K. Overbeeke, A. F. Monk, & P. C. Wright (Eds.), *Funology: From usability to enjoyment* (pp. 43–53). Dordrecht: Kluwer Academic Publishers.

Chapter 2
Theories of Experience

Abstract In order to begin the process of building a theory of UX, this chapter first lays foundations and defines key terms such as *user, technology, experience, time* and *meaning*. Specifically, experience is discussed in terms of the different ways that it may be understood, for example, as *experience*, as *an experience*, and as *co-experience*. Also, the notion of *time* is linked to experience, where time is described as *retrospective* and *introspective* time. Furthermore, *meaning* is explored in its different guises, as well as in relation to categorisation and sorting. The second part of the chapter is concerned with examining three primary ways in which user experience has been categorised and understood: as *qualities* (e.g. the qualities of a product, context or environment), as *consequences* (e.g. affect, emotion and pleasure), and as *processes* (including anticipatory, interpretive, reflective, behavioural, and visceral levels of processing). Finally, a new model for understanding UX is proposed: ICE (*Interaction, Construction*, and *Evaluation*).

Keywords Human–computer interaction (HCI) • Mobile device usability • Personal Construct Theory (PCT) • Categorisation • Sense making • Experience • User experience (UX) • User experience dynamics • Time • Meaning • ICE model • Pleasure • Affect

2.1 Foundations

Recent psychology literature has shown that researchers have directed their attention towards *positive psychology* (Kahneman et al. 1999; Seligman and Csikszentmihalyi 2000), where the focus is no longer about fixing and reducing problems, but about actively creating and promoting positive human experience. At the same time, the focus of design and research for technological products and services have also undergone gradual changes such that early emphasis was on utility and efficiency, where design was centred on interaction, usability and functionality (Norman 1990). The emphasis then shifted towards a concern for products and services that provide pleasurable experiences, such as *psychological, physiological, sociological* and *ideological* pleasures (Jordan 1999), and more recently, the attention is on emotional design (Norman 2003). These changes have been marked by the prolific use of terms such as *User Experience* (UX) in the Human–Computer Interaction (HCI) and product-design literature. This shift has also been evident in consultancy companies adopting the term.

This focus of attention has coincided with recent technological advances that create more possibilities for involving computational devices that are ever-present in people's lives (*Ubiquitous Computing*), and as the power of computer-processors improves dramatically, it has been increasingly possible to provide richer experiences for technology users. These changes have highlighted the need for a better understanding of how people experience technology, in order to help product and service designers to provide for the 'experience economy' (Pine and Gilmore 1999).

Consequently, there have been a number of attempts at understanding this seemingly nebulous notion of UX, and many have resulted in a wide range of uni-disciplinary approaches that do not take advantage of the existing knowledge-base of other disciplines. This has produced a diverse set of definitions and theories of user experience, which has led to a wide variety of directions for research regarding UX (Hassenzahl and Tractinsky 2006). However, to date, one of the main perceptions regarding the nature of UX have been that it is essentially usability, interaction design, and Information Architecture. Another view has shown UX to be usability with some extra attention given to the emotional aspects, such as fun, beauty and hedonics (Hassenzahl 2004). Equally, UX has been seen as something completely different, and is a more of holistic entity that is borne of many aspects of experience (McCarthy and Wright 2004).

This chapter examines the different theories and frameworks (a set of principles) regarding experience, and explores how such theories can be used to further understand how people experience technology. The main areas of literature that are explored here come from the fields of HCI, product-design, and psychology. In these disciplines, the notion of experience is defined and approached somewhat differently. However, in order to find common threads that bind these theories, specifically with respect to technology, this chapter is divided into three parts. First the terms 'technology' and 'experience' will be defined, in order to have a useful and workable understanding in this book. The second part will show the common theories that describe experience, in general, and specifically with technology. The concluding part of this chapter will draw on the previous sections and summarise the information into a new framework that will be used to inform further studies designed to explore how experience is related to physical and abstract qualities of technology.

2.1.1 Defining 'Experience' and 'Technology'

User experience (UX) is a term that specifically refers to the experience of users of technology. This term has been used extensively in the HCI literature since the 1970's and increasingly in the web development and product design realms (Edwards and Kasik 1974). However, before further discussion on definitions of experience, it is important to make clear what is meant by technology in the context of this book. Technology is used here to mean the practical application of scientific and engineering knowledge towards the accomplishment of a task, using mechanical or electronic means. For the purpose of grounding the discussions in this book with a specific kind of technology, the referenced research studies will be concerned with digital technology, specifically mobile digital media devices. Further, in order to have any meaningful discussion around the topic of experience, it is important to explore the different definitions of the term 'experience', and to outline a working definition of the term, in order to draw boundaries around the scope in this book.

There are several definitions of 'experience' and they tend to differ depending on the literature-base and the purpose behind the definition. In the following discussion, there will be a distinction made between 'experience' and 'an experience'. Dewey made an attempt to describe *experience* and *an experience* (1934, p. 36). He explained his distinctions where *experience* is the prosaic everyday life kind of experience and there is a lack of heightened emotional or affective state that is directly linked with that particular experience, such as sending email or using a word processor. Such an activity may well be considered mundane, and will go unnoticed. Being unnoticed could be due to habituation or familiarity, and a person may begin to notice the experience if it is stopped or if the activity's continuity is threatened in any way. For example, a person getting used to being able to use email for regular communications, or a word processor may suddenly notice these technologies if they are no longer available.

However, 'an experience' is one that stands alone, where there is a beginning, middle and an end. Cohesion is provided by an overarching affective state that spans the experience. For example, an event that touches a person's sense of values may elicit an emotional response of some kind, e.g. the first time a person sends or receives an email message. Such an experience may make a strong impression that is influenced by expectations from the user themselves or from other people, as well as the attitudes the person may have towards the technology itself. A task such as this may elicit a level of affect that depends on how it may be connected to other aspects of that person's life, as well as the motivations that are driving them towards engaging in the task. Dewey's distinctions are similar to Kahneman's (1999, p. 4) where 'instant experience' (*instant utility*) is the immediate evaluation of the current situation, e.g. "this is uncomfortable". Whereas a summation of a past experience is more of a 'retrospective experience' (*remembered utility*) that produces an evaluation of the whole experience, e.g. "I had a good time".

However, such an experience may in itself be a consummation of a particular need or desire. In the example of the email user, this could be something they have planned towards, and have finally been able to realise. Dennis and Powers (1974) discuss these *consummatory experiences* and how peak-experiences are realised when a person, for example, has an experience that consummates a self-actualising need (Maslow 1987, p. 137). They also compare this peak-experience with Dewey's *aesthetic experience*, where the aesthetic need is satisfied. Such experiences need not be an individualistic event, but could be shared with others. For example, one or more users may be using a networked application such as Instant Messenger (IM), where a shared experience is born and co-created. This is referred to as a 'co-experience', and maybe defined as "the seamless blend of user experience of products and social interaction" (Battarbee 2003, p. 109).

Another interesting aspect of experiences is the ability of people to 'own' them, cherish them or appropriate them. This aspect was explored by studying the meanings of possessions, where Richins proposed that an experience can be 'owned' and can hold value: "The 'possession' here is not so much the photograph but rather memories and experiences that cannot be bought at any price" (Richins 1994, p. 505). Therefore, in this context, an experience with technology can also have value in the sense that a person may recall the day they first flew solo in an aeroplane. In this sense, they have appropriated the experience of that special event (McCarthy and Wright 2004).

In summary then, 'experience' can be instantaneous and can be the mundane and prosaic type, while meaning or emotion may bind experience to make 'an experience', that may be recalled and summarised. Experiences can also be consummatory and can even be appropriated. Finally, experiences are not necessarily individualistic, they can also be shared and co-created.

2.1.2 Time and Experience

Time is an important concept in the context of experience, because experience always has a duration, and judgments of such a duration changes as experience unfolds. There are two types of time: *physical time*, the kind that can be measured with a clock, and *psychological time*, the kind that a person could estimate a sense of. For UX, the latter type of time is more relevant, and is explored here in the context of experience.

Empirically-based theories on how people sense time, divide psychological time into two types: *prospective* time and *retrospective* time (Zakay and Block 1997, p. 15). The prospective time paradigm is when a person is sensing time as the event unfolds, whereas retrospective time is when a person recalls an event and its sub-events to estimate time, therefore a memory related task. Prospective time was examined by Orme (1969) in his book on time, experience and behaviour. Orme used empirical data on subjective accounts of the passing of time and concluded that "'Filled' time, in fact, seems generally shorter than

'unfilled' time. The roles of motivation and expectancy also seem of importance."
(1969, p. 10). This sense of filled time is also referred to as a state of 'flow',
where "Self-consciousness disappears, and the sense of time becomes distorted."
(Csikszentmihalyi 1990, p. 71). Csikszentmihalyi also refers to this type of experience as 'optimal experience'. This special state of flow has a very similar profile to the one described by the Yerkes-Dodson (1908) law. The basic premise of
this principle is that for the state of flow to occur a person's skills and abilities
need to be challenged, but not too much, and there is an optimal channel where
this state will occur and a person is said to be 'engaged'. Therefore, flow is a
quality of prospective experience. This notion of disappearing self-consciousness
is mirrored in Norman's (1990) suggestion that a well designed user interface is
also one that disappears (the invisible computer) and all that remains is the user
engaged in the task.

Retrospective time on the other hand, as the name suggests, is sensed after the
event or experience of the event. This relationship of time and experience was
also important for Dewey. According to his view, experience always has a history, somehow: "an instantaneous experience is an impossibility" (Dewey 1934,
p. 229). Also, Hobbs, the seventeenth century philosopher suggested that time
arose from the succession of ideas (Orme 1969, p. 148). Therefore, to experience
something, there has to be some kind of relation that is established between one
instance and another, with reference to something else.

Retrospective time can also be understood using the 'contextual change' model
(Block 1990). The principle behind this model is that a person relies on the change
of context in order to sense time over a long period. Such contextual changes may
be smaller chunks within a larger task. However, if context is assumed not to be
a 'reality' but a way of organising events, then context is a construction, and it
is akin to 'understanding' the world. Kelly (1955) refers to this activity as 'construing' and proposes that people are constantly re-construing. Therefore, these
contextual changes are essentially perpetual cycles of re-construing. Kelly also
refers to experience as a construction in its own right, which is being constantly
revised. This emphasises the aspect of time as an integral part of experience. He
defines experience as "a matter of successively construing events" (1955, p. 65).
Therefore, according to Kelly, to have more experience is to go through the sub-
units of this cycle, i.e. to do more construing. Eventually, a person may 'take
stock', i.e. make sense of a whole group of contextual changes, in order to make
meaning. Further, according to Kelly's Personal Construct Theory (PCT), the
notion of meaning is tightly connected with that of time, he states that "The meaning of an event—that is to say, the meaning we ascribe to it—is anchored in its
antecedents and it consequents. Thus meaning displays itself to us mainly in the
dimension of time" (Kelly 2003, p. 4). The temporal nature of experience is therefore seen as integral aspect of experience. Experience is seen as the serialisation of
psychological events, otherwise known as *experience events*. The sense of looking
ahead, and bringing previous experiences to bear on new upcoming experiences
is a key aspect of sensing time and experience. As Kelly puts it, experience has
units or quanta, where "The unit of experience is, therefore, a cycle embracing five

phases: anticipation, investment, encounter, confirmation or disconfirmation, and constructive revisions" (Kelly 2003, p. 12).

To summarise, there are important distinctions and parallels between the natures of time and experience. The suggestion is that experience has a dual nature. The first is the *prospective experience*, which is an immediate processing of a continuous sense of time, as in Dewey's *experience*. However, the other nature of experience is that of a *retrospective experience* which is the result of understanding contextual changes, as described by the constancy in re-construing between 'units of experience', to create a whole. This is what Dewey calls *an experience* and is akin to *understanding* (Butt 2004). The former feeds the latter to create a whole, that ultimately builds a perpetual connectedness of past, present and future. This connectedness is ultimately, the foundry of meaning.

2.1.3 Categorisation, Making-Sense, and Meaning

In order to have a sense of contextual changes, a person must be able to distinguish between contexts, in other words, be able to categorise them. Lakoff (1987) expresses the importance of categorisation in how people understand the world around them. He makes it clear that "categorization is not a matter to be taken lightly. There is nothing more basic than categorization to our thought, perception, action and speech" (Lakoff 1987, p. 5). Categorisation is also a way of making meaning visible. Kaplan and Kaplan (1989) argued that people's perception and categorisation are the mechanisms that are used to create meaning. They state that "people react to what they experience in terms of commonalities, in terms of classes or categories. A scene is generally perceived as a particular instance of a larger class of scenes" (Kaplan and Kaplan 1989, p. 20).

However, it is important to remember that such categorisations are not 'real', they are constructions, and can be operationalised via 'constructs'. The central precept of Kelly's PCT is the 'construct', which is akin to the criteria a person may use to understand or distinguish a stimulus from other stimuli. Therefore, it could be argued that the building blocks of how users understand and make sense of their world are their constructs. A construct is defined as "a way in which some things are construed as being alike and yet different from others" (Kelly, 1955, p. 74). Therefore, in Kelly's theory, constructs are what people use to make sense of their world around them as they experience it. Kelly also points out the dynamic nature of constructs, and emphasises this aspect as fundamental to what experience is. Thus "as one's anticipations or hypotheses are successively revised in the light of the unfolding sequence of events, the construction system undergoes a progressive evolution. The person reconstrues. This is experience" (Kelly 1955, p. 51).

For Kelly, these constructs come about through the creative interpretation of successive cycles of experience, whereby earlier constructs are overturned quite naturally by later ones. He refers to this process as one of 'constructive alternativism', which is the opposite of 'accumulative fragmentalism', or the collection of truth piece by piece. This process is also called 're-construing' and "by construing we mean 'placing an interpretation'… the substance takes shape or assumes meaning" (Kelly 1955, p. 35). Since 'to construe' is to make meaning, and construing and re-construing is a constant process that makes experience, meaning is therefore a central concept of experience. However, "there are at least as many meanings of 'meaning' as there are disciplines which deal with language" (Osgood et al. 1957, p. 2). Importantly though, meaning is distinguishable from association: "an association is not meaning, it is merely a link from one representation in memory to another" (Johnson-Laird 1988, p. 99). Therefore, for the purpose of this analysis, meaning is defined as "semantical meaning—the relation of signs to their significates .., that distinctive meditational process or state which is occurs in the organism whenever a sign is received" (Osgood et al. 1957, p. 3). Meaning can therefore be partly defined as the 'state' or response it elicits in a person making meaning. Ultimately, a person's attribution of meaning gives rise to their affective and behavioural responses. In the examples above, the meanings have the potential to have a profound effect on the experience that a user may have with a technological device. These meanings, however, are not static. They are dynamic in the sense that the current experience will serve to influence the next experience, and create yet another meaning.

This progressive evolution of the construction system is essentially the sense-making process that is central to Kelly's theory. This is where a person makes-sense of events by re-construing the events in the light of existing constructs, and perhaps finding alternative constructs that better fit the 'data'. Of course, in this case the data are the 'whole' data, not just the event itself, i.e. all of their past relevant experiences. In this way, for Kelly (1955, p. 65), a person will use the "stock-taking" process in order to make-sense and then attribute meaning to a psychological event. However, these events and experiences that are being re-construed are not seen here as 'real' but as the person's point of view. This is where Kelly's theory is also grounded in Dewey's pragmatic philosophy. This pragmatic point of view emphasises the role of the subjective view of what a person perceives, as the view that matters. This is directly related to phenomenology, which is the study of phenomena, the world as it appears to a person, or as they experience it (Husserl 1931). This is in contrast to what the world 'really is', which is a world people can never know. However, since Kelly's theory emphasises the person's view, it is therefore fundamentally, a phenomenological theory (Butt 2008).

2.2 Theories of User Experience

2.2.1 Experience as Qualities

Different areas of HCI have taken different points of view regarding what the term *User Experience* (UX) means, and some may argue that current business usage of this term is simply usability guidelines executed correctly

(ISO-9241-11 1998). Some practitioner-based views prefer to focus on a task-based definition, for example the "general categories of work (required to) create a user experience... *information architecture... interaction design... identity design*" (Kuniavsky 2003, p. 44). Nonetheless, early effort towards operationalising the term, started with a list of criteria that defined '*qualities of experience*' that could be used to judge the extent interactive products provide a good experience (Alben 1996), defining experience as "all the aspects of how people use an interactive product: the way it feels in their hands, how well they understand how it works, how they feel about it while they're using it, how well it serves their purposes, and how well it fits into the entire context in which they are using it" (Alben 1996, p. 12). Alben defines the quality of experience in terms of factors that either *contribute to experience* or are *components of experience*. These factors were derived by an open discussion of industry experts that would subsequently use these criteria to judge the extent that a product is well designed for a good experience. The criteria fall in two groups: ones that are related to the development process of a product, and ones that contribute directly to the experience. Understanding the user and having an effective design process are seen as qualities of the design process. However, making sure the product is learnable and usable, as well as appropriate to the task were part of the qualities that contribute directly to the experience. In this category, Alben also included the aesthetic aspects of the product, as well as the adaptability of the product in terms of being flexible to address the needs of the user. These guidelines showed a wide and ill-defined scope and criteria. However, they were seen as a starting point for discussion on what experience really means. Importantly, these 'qualities' are loose themes, and heuristics, and no attempt was made to explain their theoretical or indeed empirical basis.

Jääskö and Mattelmäki (2003) went further, and proposed a list of elements that were seen as aspects of the experience rather than design goals. They saw the qualities of user experience to be divided into two parts (Fig. 2.1). One part relates to the product itself (top two qualities in Fig. 2.1), such as *appearance* and the *user interface*. The second part (bottom five qualities in Fig. 2.1) consists of aspects external to the product, but have an influence on the experience as a whole. The qualities in this second group relate to what the user brings to the scene: their personality, self-image, expectations (including novelty), values and beliefs. Meaning is also in this group, as it is something that a user will create and attach to a product or device, and this will depend on past experiences with sociological and physical contexts. The physical interaction with the product is also highlighted as an aspect of the quality of experience. These qualities were derived from their review of the relevant literature at the time, and then summarised into a usable list of qualities.

In establishing the above list of the qualities of user experience, Jääskö and Mattelmäki were able to suggest experimental methods that were used to investigate these aspects, such as cultural probes and observation (Gaver et al. 1999). They undertook two case-studies to investigate experience: one in a laboratory setting and the other in a hospital. Their results showed that combining these two

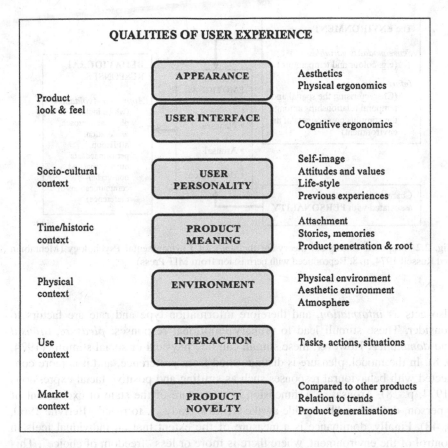

QUALITIES OF USER EXPERIENCE

Product look & feel	APPEARANCE	Aesthetics Physical ergonomics
	USER INTERFACE	Cognitive ergonomics
Socio-cultural context	USER PERSONALITY	Self-image Attitudes and values Life-style Previous experiences
Time/historic context	PRODUCT MEANING	Attachment Stories, memories Product penetration & root
Physical context	ENVIRONMENT	Physical environment Aesthetic environment Atmosphere
Use context	INTERACTION	Tasks, actions, situations
Market context	PRODUCT NOVELTY	Compared to other products Relation to trends Product generalisations

Fig. 2.1 Qualities of user experience (Reproduced with permission from Jääskö and Mattelmäki 2003)

experimental methods would allow access to data pertaining to each of the aspects they describe. However, a possible criticism of this list is the subjective nature of its derivation from a reduced literature review, however, it makes a good list for HCI practitioners and designers to have a potentially useful heuristic framework for paying attention to aspects of UX. Also, this list did not include any information regarding the dynamic nature of UX, and how these elements may change for a user over time.

2.2.2 Experience as Consequences

In the environmental psychology literature, a simple model of how people interact with the environment was proposed by Mehrabian and Russell (1974, p. 8) (Fig. 2.2). The model proposes the environment as a stimulus via the different modalities of the senses (visual, auditory, kinaesthetic etc.). The environment

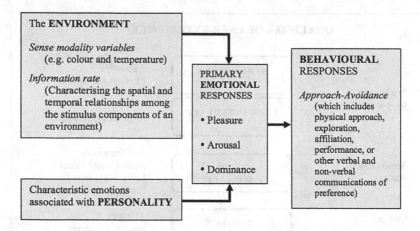

Fig. 2.2 Proposed conceptual theory for the study of Environmental Psychology (Mehrabian and Russell 1974, p. 8. Reproduced with permission from MIT Press)

also acts as *information*, and therefore information type and rate are factors to consider. These stimuli lead to primary emotional responses: *pleasure, arousal* and *dominance*. However, these stimuli can be "physical or social stimuli" (1974, p. 8). In the model, pleasure is distinguished from preference, and it is more connected with behavioural responses such as smiling and positive facial expressions (1974, p. 18). Arousal as a dimension is a measure of the state of excitement of a person, defined as "how wide awake ... how ready ... to react" (Berlyne 1960, p. 48). Finally, dominance is a measure of the extent that an individual feels in control of the environment, where there is more or less "freedom of choice". This is marked by the individual's feeling that there is no restriction to the ways that he or she is able to act (1974, p. 19). All the above dimensions of the primary emotional response are underlined by the emotional characteristics, related to the person's personality and individual differences.

This model focuses on the end result of stimuli from the environment, and recognises that the stimuli can be direct sensorial types or social (i.e. semantic) stimuli. Information rate is seen as a property of the environmental stimulus, and this too can be semantic information as well as sensorial information. However, the focus of this model is the consequence of such stimuli in terms of the affective or emotional response. The end result of an interaction of stimuli and responses is the behavioural response of a person, i.e. what they will do, in the sense of an *approach-avoidance* response. As a first approximation, this model fits well in the context of technology, if technology is seen as 'the environment'. As will be discussed later, the perception of the environment is an important aspect of experiencing technology, as well as the way information is being processed, e.g. how *complex* the scene is, how *coherent*, and how *typical* is the stimulus. This is a cognitive model that shows the stimulus, i.e. the environment, as deterministic without taking into account the constructive aspects of the emotional responses. The processes that lead to the emotional responses are therefore too narrowly defined.

However, emotions and the notion of pleasure have been explored in many ways. Ultimately, it is a manifestation of the evaluation that a person may have when experiencing. Berlyne discusses it in the sense of behavioural pleasure that can be measured in terms of "verbal, facial or postural responses" (1973, p. 11). Others have expressed it in terms of a subjective entity that may be understood from a phenomenological standpoint (Duncker 1941). However, recent efforts have focused on defining this term in such a way as to allow empirical measurement and study with respect to products. In his book "The pursuit of pleasure", Tiger (1992), classifies pleasure into four types, and he demonstrates how this categorisation works to help understand general human behaviour. Jordan (1999) used these categories to analyse how these pleasures specifically apply to HCI, technology and products in general. The definition that Jordan uses is that "Pleasure with products: The emotional, hedonic and practical benefits associated with products" (Jordan 1999, p. 12). Therefore, for Jordan, pleasure with products may be categorised into the following four pleasures: *physiological, psychological, sociological* and *ideological*.

The *physiological* pleasures are associated with the sensual elements, such as tactile and visceral kinds of interactions, or the colour or shape. For example, the touch and the weight of an object can instil a particular satisfaction, and if an object feels lighter or heavier than expected or anticipated, then this can cause negative affect or a pleasant surprise, depending on the context. *Psychological* pleasures are linked to cognitive and emotional activities and are derived when a person is able to take part in activities that engender positive cognitive or emotional engagement. For example a person may enjoy playing chess or working out how to fix a broken device. Equally, a creative activity such as painting or writing would give psychological pleasure. The *sociological* pleasure is derived from situations where a person's social needs are met or highlighted, such as having coffee with friends, or going to a music concert. Social pleasure is also gained when an object is used as a talking point that allows a person to interact with others. Finally, when a person's beliefs or values are operationalised, they gain *ideological* pleasure. For example, using an energy-saving car for a person that believes in environmental conservation, will give them pleasure. Or conversely, cruising on an open highway in a large powerful car, would give pleasure to the person that values travel and freedom.

However, with a focus on the hedonic aspects of experience, a further development of the above model by Mehrabian and Russell (1974) was proposed by Hassenzahl and Tractinsky (2006), when they defined user experience as a "consequence of a user's internal state ... the characteristics of the designed system ... and the context (or the environment) within which the interaction occurs" (2006, p. 95). In their definition, the 'consequence', i.e. an end-point, and the 'internal state' can be seen as a mixture of the 'behavioural response' and 'primary emotional responses' in Fig. 2.2, whereas the 'designed system' is akin to the 'environment'. However, this definition hints towards the constructive elements of experience by acknowledging the 'context' and its related concepts such as meaning. However, although Hassenzahl and Tractinsky describe user experience as having 'facets': *beyond the instrumental, emotion & affect,* and *the experiential* (2006), these may be seen as categories of experience.

The above facets are also described by Hassenzahl and Tractinsky as 'perspectives' of experience. In other words types or examples of experience. The first perspective, *beyond instrumental,* refers to the experiences users have that are not related to the functionality of the technology, but with such aspects as aesthetics and hedonics. For example, a mobile telephone may well function according to technical requirements, but the user expects more than this (Norman 2003). The expectation is for the telephone to provide an aesthetic experience. The second perspective is one of *emotion and affect.* This can be seen as an evaluative part of what is being experienced, which of course feeds back into the experience itself, or a new experience. For example, a user can derive an experience that mediates a positive emotional state when communicating with a missed family member, using video conferencing technology. The third perspective is related to *the experiential* aspect. This distinction initially comes across as self-referential. However, what is meant by this is that the experiential aspect refers specifically to the temporal and dynamic dimensions, as well as the spatial and conceptual context. An example of this kind of perspective would be a person that uses a particular device such as a new MP3 player. The person will have anticipations, goals, motivations and expectations. These internal states will be bracketed by the beginning and end of the experience as well as the spatial context.

Further, Hassenzahl and Tractinsky (2006), advocate that empirical research methods must be developed in order to investigate these facets, and they refer to a few examples of studies that show progress towards building research tools to investigate these perspectives. However, this model essentially advocates the study of different *types* of experiences (e.g. experiences that are "aesthetic", "positive", or "unique"), rather than make an attempt at theorising on the *nature* of user experience itself.

2.2.3 Experience as Processes

So far, the models discussed above have focused on the general quality of experience or the different types of experience. However, Norman (2003) proposed a cognitive model that suggests different ways of processing of sensorial stimuli (Fig. 2.3). These stimuli lead to evaluative judgements, which eventually show up as emotion (see the link between environment and response in Fig. 2.2). Norman's model considers three primary levels of processing of people's interactions with products: *visceral, behavioural* and *reflective.* The visceral level is where it is entirely related to the senses and how people may evaluate such stimuli at a sensorial level. Zajonc (1980) has shown that people are able to process at this level faster than they can with any reflective or cognitive level.

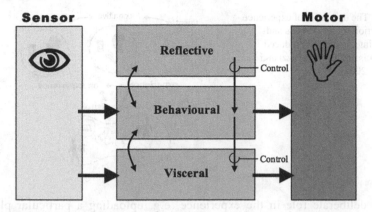

Fig. 2.3 Levels of processing (Reproduced with permission from Norman 2003, p. 22)

The behavioural level is the kind of processing that requires a learned skill of some kind, like driving a car or operating a machine. The cognitive or reflective level is where users are required to think about or make conscious effort to "work out" what is required to be done, in any particular situation. Norman makes a clear distinction between cognition and affect, such that "cognition interprets the world, leading to increased understanding and knowledge. Affect, which includes emotion, is a system of judging what's good or bad, safe or dangerous. It makes value judgements, the better to survive" (Norman 2003, p. 20).

This distinction between the thinking and feeling, is based on Zajonc's work (1980). However, such cognitive models have been criticised as reductive, where the "richness of emotion in interaction mitigates against reductive representation" (Boehner et al. 2007, p. 289). Light acknowledges this criticism by researchers who "reject a reductive approach" (Light 2006, p. 187), favouring a more interpretive methodology for research. Other models have focused their attention on the holistic nature of experience, rather than a consequence or outcome, and have shown it as a process or relationships. One such point of view was illustrated by the relational model given by Forlizzi and Ford (2000), where they saw experience as the relationship between the user and the object in the scope of the context that underlies this relationship (Fig. 2.6). This is similar to the view held by Falk and Dierking (1992), where experience is described as an interaction of *personal*, *physical* and *social contexts*. However, as mentioned earlier, the use of 'context' has a strong constructive element. Forlizzi and Ford's (2000) somewhat constructivist perspective was later developed into a more elaborate model of user experience that also takes account of the changes that occur over time (Forlizzi and Battarbee 2004). In other words, the dynamics of the experience are now seen as a fundamental aspect of user experience (Fig. 2.4). They show that experiences with products can be 'fluent' where the person is not thinking about what they are doing, e.g. a typist using a keyboard. However, an experience can also be 'expressive' where the person

Fig. 2.4 The dynamics of experience
in interaction for individuals and
in social interaction (Reproduced
with permission from Forlizzi and
Battarbee 2004)

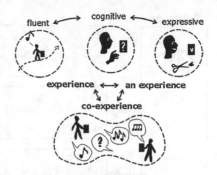

takes a deliberate role in the experience, e.g. uploading a particular playlist
in an MP3 player. Alternatively, an experience can be 'cognitive', which is
between the former types, where the user is working through some task, e.g.
working out how to use a new device. However, what Forlizzi and Battarbee
add to Dewey's 'experience' and 'an experience' is the 'co-experience' that any
of the above types of user-product experiences can also be. In other words, a
person can have fluent, cognitive or expressive experiences not just by themselves, but with others too. As Hassenzahl and Tractinsky (2006) did, this new
theory also proposed 'types' of experience. However, these types are organised
in a more categorical manner, rather than the exemplars of the earlier theory.
The first is *experience*, which is where a person is engaged in a constant stream
of self-talk. The second is *an experience*, where the experience is episodic in
the sense that it has a beginning, middle and end (similar to the *experiential*
aspect of Hassenzahl and Tractinsky). The third type is a *co-experience*, where
the experience is shared and mediated by a product use (Fig. 2.4).

Interestingly, this theory highlights the temporal nature of experience, as well
as the relational and contextual aspect. These are key aspects of sense-making, and
are illustrated in a philosophical capacity. However, what is missing is the psychological description of how the user makes sense of these aspects. Sense making is
the focus of two theories of experience reviewed next.

A framework that focuses on the processes involved in user experience was
proposed by McCarthy and Wright (2004). They proposed a two-part framework
grounded in the pragmatic philosophy of Dewey (1934) and Bakhtin (1984),
where a defining point of view is that the person's sense of the world is the one
that matters, not a reality that can never be known. This philosophy also brings
Bakhtin's notion of 'unfinalisability' of experience. The idea that experience is
something that is forever unfolding and evolving, by a constancy of processes.
McCarthy and Wright propose a view of "technology as experience", where people's relationship with technology is understood phenomenologically, from the
perspective of a user's active, on-going and creative attempts to incorporate it
into everyday life. For them, researchers "should try to interpret the relationship
between people and technology in terms of the felt life and the felt or emotional
quality of action and interaction" (2004, p. 12).

They describe 'felt life' as the sense that "felt experience points to the emotional and sensual quality of experience" (2004, p. 13). Further, they present their framework as a metaphor of four basic 'threads' of experience to give experience its quality: *Compositional, Emotional, Sensual* and *Spatio-Temporal*. For the *compositional* thread, they refer to the context as a whole and how all the components fit together for the person undergoing the experience, i.e. a person may feel a sense of how the experience makes sense as part of a narrative and how the pieces make up the whole. For example, when a student uses a computer to write an essay, that essay is part of the assignment they have for a particular study module, and the computer itself is part of the toolkit they have in order to complete the whole course, or it may be seen as the gift they had from their mother.

In terms of the *emotional* thread, the emphasis is on the aspects that the evaluative result of the experience in terms of the emotion a person is feeling. For example, a user of a computer-mediated game, may feel a sense of excitement and fun, or anxiety. *Sensual* threads of experience are simply the direct sensory inputs that a user has when experiencing a technological device; its textural feel, colour, weight, temperature etc. These sensual feelings are pre-reflective (Zajonc 1980). Finally, for the *spatio-temporal* thread, McCarthy and Wright refer to the physical space and time where the experience is taking place, where the feeling of the space may change; narrow down or open up, and the sense of time may speed up and slow down.

McCarthy and Wright pointed out that these threads are seen as interleaved and not be taken as "fundamental elements of experience", but should be taken as "ideas to help us think clearly about technology as experience" (2004, p. 79). Although using a metaphor of 'threads in a braid' may be useful, these 'ideas' could be classified as properties of experience, or manifestations and consequences of people having experience.

In the second part of their framework, McCarthy and Wright (2004) refer to the processes that people use to make sense of their experience with technology (Fig. 2.5). The processes are not intended to be sequential or causal, and the following quotations for each process are from McCarthy and Wright (2003, p. 42). *Anticipating*: "We never come to technology unprejudiced", and in that way people anticipate upcoming events with past experiences and expectations. These expectation are also mixed with anticipations of how an event will unfold, be it a social interaction or an interaction with technology. *Connecting*: "We make a judgment in an instant and without much thought". People make connections that are pre-linguistic and pre-conceptual, and they make them in an instant. This is similar to associations. *Interpreting*: "We work out what's going on and how we feel about it". This is also a matter of 'discerning' the structure of a narrative, including what is about to happen, not just what happened. *Reflecting*: "We examine and evaluate what is happening in an interaction". This process involves making judgements about aspects of the unfolding experience, including relating events to motivations and anticipations. *Appropriating*: "We work out how a new experience fits with other experiences we have had and with our sense of self". This process relates to the sense of ownership of experiences and making them

Fig. 2.5 A framework for
sense making processes,
where the four "threads of
experience" are shown in
the *centre*: compositional,
emotional, sensual and
spatio-temporal (Reproduced
with permission from
McCarthy and Wright 2003)

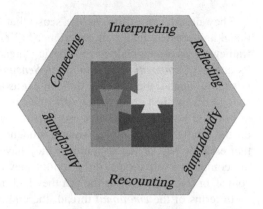

part of the unfolding narrative. *Recounting*: "We enjoy storytelling and make sense
of experience in stories". This is the process of retelling the narrative to one's
self and others. This process is related to the compositional 'thread' in the sense
that it relates the experience to other experiences. Although, the six processes are
described individually above, they can be "difficult to distinguish between some of
the sense-making processes, for example, interpreting and reflecting" (McCarthy
et al. 2005, p. 1). Therefore, although, this framework can be useful in thinking
about user experience, it can be difficult to operationalise.

McCarthy and Wright highlighted 'anticipation' as one of the processes of
sense making, but they had not connected this process with Kelly's PCT. For
Kelly, this is a fundamental process that is responsible for how people experience
their world. This process is so important for Kelly, that it holds a special place in
the main postulate of the PCT, where he asserts that "A person's processes are psychologically channelized by the ways in which he anticipates events" (Kelly 1955,
p. 32). By this, he means that the rest of the processes that a person may undergo
will follow the anticipations that the person had brought to the event. For example, if a person anticipates difficulty ahead, they may enter that situation already
tense, and looking to be on their guard. Such a situation may then exhibit confirmation bias (Mynatt et al. 1977). For Kelly, such anticipations are born of the
re-construing process, that is responsible for the constructs themselves. Further,
it is the "successive construing and re-construing" (Kelly 1955, p. 52) and sense-
making that is the essence of experience. Butt makes Kelly's equation explicit, by
stating that he deliberately uses "the phrase 'making sense of', because it is at the
heart of the Kellian project" (Butt 2008, p. 132).

Therefore, this constancy of re-construing *is* the sense-making process, where
a person may understand events in relation to other events and other constructs,
and *the more a person re-construes, the more they experience*. PCT does not enter-
tain the cognition/affect duality, and construing is "not an exclusively cognitive
process" (Butt 2008, p. 60). They only make sense in 'action', i.e. in the way people anticipate events, situated in the environment they live in, not separate from
it. This is not to say however, that understanding is some cognitive or reflective

Fig. 2.6 A theory of experience (Reproduced with permission from Forlizzi and Ford 2000)

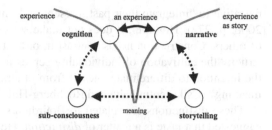

activity. Dilthey (1988) made a clear distinction between causal explanation (akin to reflective or cognitive activity) and understanding. Understanding is intimately connected to the construct making process that a person uses to make sense of their world (Butt 2004). The 'threads' that McCarthy and Wright refer to are therefore a consequence of sense-making, not the other way around, e.g. 'Emotion' is a result of re-construing. Butt again re-affirms the PCT view, stating that "disturbances in sense-making lead to a variety of states that we call emotional" (Butt 2008, p. 48).

One particular model that focused on the sense-making aspect of experience from the narrative and meaning point of view, was that proposed by Forlizzi and Ford (2000). In this model, there is a separation of *user* and *product*, which are seen as the primary components that influence experience. Interaction itself is not seen as a component. The product, which has physical attributes like shape and size, as well as features, also has tacit features that are communicated through its form, and aesthetic qualities, and perceived usefulness. The user on the other hand brings prior experiences, values and emotions to the relationship with the product. This relationship is underscored by the context of use, and then by social and cultural factors.

Forlizzi and Ford's model describes four different types of experience (Fig. 2.6). Sub-conscious experiences that are automatic and do not require any conscious cognitive activity, such as a proficient typist using on a keyboard, thus being involved in mundane *experience*. Cognitive activity is then involved in understanding and attributing meaning to experiences that require a user to think about the task, and they would be more aware of *an experience*. The accumulation of such experiences are then woven into a story as part of creating a narrative of the user's life. In this model, meaning is created when a user links individual episodes to create the story.

However, these narratives are not constructed in isolation of the environment in terms of social influences. For example, marketing efforts particularly take advantage of such influences by using the notion of brand personality "the personality consumers interpret from a specific brand" (Blackwell et al. 2006, p. 273). Such branding relies on trait-factor theory (see Chamorro-Premuzic 2007, p. 15), which suggests that people have traits that are enduring differences between individuals, e.g. sociability, risk-taking and self-consciousness. The brand is then marketed in such a way as to attribute these traits to the brand or product. The consumers are then attracted to such products in order to construct their own narrative to "integrate their past, present and anticipated future" (Blackwell et al. 2006, p. 272). However, it does not make sense to construct the self in isolation of others. Construction needs contrast in order to have meaning, as does any construct: "the cultivation of individuality serves a larger goal of integration because the intention to differentiate oneself from others still needs other people to give it meaning" (Csikszentmihalyi and Rochberg-Halton 1981, p. 33).

These distinctions are related to Bourdieu's (1984) discussiosssn of taste. He suggested that taste is a matter of *distinction*. He also proposed that people's tastes in lifestyle, activities, ideas and objects are a matter of social hierarchy, and serve the purpose of reinforcing social structure. Therefore, an individual may unknowingly *like* something just because it distinguishes them *away* from a social culture or class, and *towards* another, more desirable group. However, when their choice in a particular object (for example a type of music player like the iPod) is over-run by a group of people that they do not wish to be associated with, their taste will tend to change yet again in order to distinguish themselves from the undesirable group.

Equally, sometimes people conform or align themselves to general or peer opinion (Asch 1951), and recent experimental evidence shows that people also take-on new beliefs to conform with peer beliefs (Berns et al. 2005). Such changes in opinion can also be seen as gradual changes in preference as a result of systematic influence over long-term exposure. Such influences can also be seen as part of cultural views and representations. For example, cultural differences have been shown to be significant for interface design (Evers and Day1997), and are therefore, a factor to consider when investigating experience with technology. Equally, culturally embedded norms are important, and are sometimes referred to as 'design patterns' (see ui-patterns.com), where such differences warrant different approaches to design (Lidwell et al. 2003), as well as usability and user research (Al-Azzawi 2010).

In summary then, Kelly's PCT makes it clear what is meant by 'experience', provides a well-developed psychology theory along with a rich set of methods for investigating experience, which is also in harmony with Dewey's phenomenological stance. This makes it a useful theory for investigating specific experiences with technology.

As discussed above, PCT may be read in many ways. Two readings are of interest in this book, and a clear distinction should be made here. First, PCT may be usefully employed to describe the *constructs* that people use in the way they act in the world, where constructs are what makes two things the same, and different to another. And secondly, a person *reconstrues* events as an on-going process to experience the world, where experience cycles are "a matter of successively construing events" (Kelly 1955, p. 65). The first reading can come across as the more 'cognitive' reading, although Kelly would disagree against such a label because he was vehemently against the dualist division of mind/body, and did not see such a distinction to be a useful one. For Kelly, constructs are what people use to act in the world, not to think about it. The second reading however, takes on a more phenomenological approach to experience, and takes the person's view and re-construal of events to be the one that matters. Butt (2004) takes these two readings as a way to distinguish between 'understanding' and 'explaining'. He makes the distinction as "Personal construct psychology can be read either as an attempt to understand people by appreciating how the world appears to them, or to explain their behaviour in terms of personal constructs that inhabit some interior Cartesian realm" (Butt 2004, p. 21).

As Butt argues for both readings being contemporaneously useful in a research setting, this book also follows the same argument, and will use the readings in each study appropriately. One of the useful aspects of constructs is their apparent objectivity, i.e. they can be articulated in a clear and non-ambiguous manner, which lends them to being naturally useful in an empirical setting. This means that "PCT's methodology can be seen as providing a sort of psychic X-ray, in which an individual's system of internal constructs is revealed and can then be the focus of therapeutic attention" (Butt 2004, p. 24). Of course, this book is not intended to provide for therapy, but is nonetheless intended to provide a focus on the 'lived' experience with technology, and to reify such experiences in such a way as to provide further understanding of how people experience technology. Also, from a design point of view, 'objective' constructs, e.g. colour or size, may be used towards a 'shared' world between designer and user, although only the meaning attributed by the user is the useful one to the user.

From the above discussion regarding the nature of experience, and more specifically *user experience*, it can be seen that the term itself is a complex construct, like 'intelligence', where in fact there are many processes that contribute to what people might call 'experience', and only a specifically constructed and defined term with a specified set of processes and mechanisms may then become useful to study and explore. Therefore, experience will be defined by a new framework termed *ICE*, where the *Constructive* processes are the glue of experience, and they create the interfaces with the 'real world' through the *Interactive* process, where the consequences are made visible or felt by the *Evaluative* responses. This essentially asynchronous process (not sequential or linear) is explained in the next section.

2.2.4 ICE: Processes of User Experience

Taking into account the review of the theories discussed above in several disciplines (e.g. HCI, product design, environmental psychology, and social psychology), the processes of UX may be classified into three categories (Fig. 2.7):

Interaction is the first category. For the purpose of this book, the primary aspects of interaction are defined as 'action' and 'perception' (visual and other sensory stimuli), between the user and technology (Norman 2003). Action refers to the user somehow controlling the technology to achieve a desired goal. The perceptual aspect is concerned with what the user perceives directly and how they understand what they perceive. Perception could be categorised into two types.

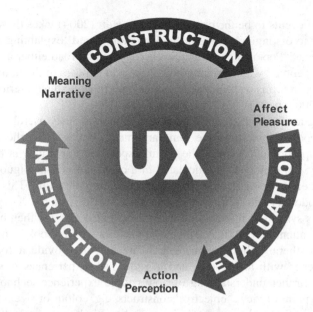

Fig. 2.7 ICE: the dynamic processes of user experience (*UX*)

The first is 'remote perception', where the viewer does not see themselves as 'part of the environment', but an onlooker who is separate from it. Remote perception may be seen as either the physical sensory impression creating a physiological response, or some basic level of sensory information processing such as novelty. The second type of perception is 'ecological perception' where the viewer perceives the environment with a degree of engagement and appreciation of their place in it, and the intentions they have in it (Gibson 1979). Only ecological perception will be of interest in this book.

   Construction is the second category of UX processes, and is a fundamental process for experience, which serves to make experience what it is, in terms of how a person understands it. Construction therefore, has a primary effect on experience, as well as meaning, such as private and public meanings, and how a user has a meaningful relationship with technological devices. Narratives, the stories, are also influenced by construction, where users tell themselves about how the experience fits in with other experiences and their life in general, including their sense of time. Also, construction is key to how a user conceptualises and understands their environment as they interact with it. Construction therefore, refers to the idea of people creating their conceptualisation of their world around them and making meaning. The concept of a 'construct' as used in this book is aligned with Kelly's definition, which is a person's sense of what makes something different to something else, yet the same as another. This category will be the focus of much of the research. Meaning, and its different types, will be discussed in the next chapter.

Evaluation is the third category of UX processes. This category encompasses evaluative responses or consequence of experience, i.e. how the user feels about it. It can also include physiological responses as well as reflective, affective and emotional evaluations. Aesthetics responses, as well as the types of pleasure that a user feels when interacting with technology are also part of this category of ICE. The following chapter will investigate how people evaluate external stimuli as well as internal constructions such as meaning and narrative. These stimuli and constructions ultimately influence their experience with technology.

In this chapter, the notion of experience was initially explored, and then the link between time and experience was illustrated. Specifically, the term *user experience* was then discussed using particular theories. These theories were seen to focus on *qualities*, *consequences* or *processes* as ways of defining UX. Also, the three fundamental processes of UX were highlighted in a simple framework, *ICE: interaction, construction* and *evaluation*. This chapter also raises two key questions for this research area. The first is about how people make meaning through their User Experience and iterations within ICE. The second is a about the key constructs in people's User Experience. The next chapter explores empirical studies that measure aspects of ICE, showing evidence of their involvement in User Experience, and are helpful towards answering the above questions.

References

Al-Azzawi, A. (2010). User research throughout the world: United Arab emirates. In R. M. Schumacher (Ed.), *Handbook of global user research*. Burlington: Morgan Kaufman.

Alben, L. (1996). Quality of experience: Defining the criteria for effective interaction design. *Interactions, 3*(3), 11–15.

Asch, S. E. (1951). Effects of group pressure upon the modification and distortion of judgments. In H. S. Guetzkow (Ed.), *Leadership and men research in human relations* (pp. 177–190). Pittsburgh: Carnegie Press.

Bakhtin, M. (1984). *Problems of Dostoevsky's poetics*. Minnesota: University of Minnesota Press.

Battarbee, K. (2003). *Defining co-experience*. Paper presented at the Proceedings of Conference on Designing Pleasurable Products and Interfaces, Pittsburgh.

Berlyne, D. E. (1960). *Conflict, arousal and curiosity*. New York: McGraw-Hill.

Berlyne, D. E. (1973). The vicissitudes of aplopathematic and thelematoscopic pneumatology (or The hydrography of hedonism). In D. E. Berlyne & K. B. Madsen (Eds.), *Pleasure, reward, preference: Their nature, determinants and role in behavior* (pp. 1–33). New York: Academic Press.

Berns, G. S., Chappelow, J. C., Zink, C. F., Pagnoni, G., Martin-Skurski, M. E., & Richards, R. (2005). Neurobiological correlates of social conformity and independence during mental rotation. *Biological Psychiatry, 58*, 245–253.

Blackwell, R. D., Miniard, P. W., & Engel, J. F. (2006). *Consumer behaviour: International student edition* (Vol. 10). Mason OH: Thompson.

Block, R. A. (1990). Models of psychological time. In R. A. Block, (Ed.), *Cognitive models of psychological time* (pp. 1–35). Hillsdale, NJ: Erlbaum.

Boehner, K., DePaula, R., Dourish, P., & Sengers, P. (2007). How emotion is made and measured. *International Journal of Human-Computer Studies, 65*, 275–291.

Bourdieu, P. (1984). *Distinction: A social critique of the judgement of taste*. London: Routledge.

Butt, T. (2004). Understanding, explanation and personal constructs. *Personal Construct Theory & Practice, 1*, 21–27.

Butt, T. (2008). *George Kelly: The psychology of personal constructs*. Basingstoke: Palgrave Macmillan.

Chamorro-Premuzic, T. (2007). *Personality and individual differences*. Oxford: BPS Blackwell.

Csikszentmihalyi, M. (1990). *Flow: The psychology of optimal experience*. New York: Harper Collins.

Csikszentmihalyi, M., & Rochberg-Halton, E. (1981). *The meaning of things*. Cambridge: Cambridge University Press.

Dennis, L. J., & Powers, J. F. (1974). Dewey, Maslow, and Consummatory Experience. *Journal of Aesthetic Education, 8*(4), 51-63.

Dewey, J. (1934). *Art as Experience* (paperback 2005 ed.). Perigee.

Dilthey, W. (1988). *Introduction to the human sciences: An attempt to lay a foundation for the study of society and history*. Detroit: Wayne State University Press.

Duncker, K. (1941). On pleasure, emotion and striving. *Philosophy and phenomenological research, 1*, 391–430.

Edwards, E. C., & Kasik, D. J. (1974). *User experience with the CYBER graphics terminal*. Paper presented at the Proceedings of VIM-21.

Evers, V., & Day, D. (1997). The role of culture in interface acceptance. In S. Howard, J. Hammond & G. Lindgaard (Eds.), *Proceedings of Human Computer Interaction INTERACT'97*. London: Chapman and Hall.

Falk, J. H., & Dierking, L. D. (1992). *The museum experience*. Washington: Howells House.

Forlizzi, J., & Battarbee, K. (2004). *Understanding experience*. Paper presented at the Proceedings of DIS 2004, New York.

Forlizzi, J., & Ford, S. (2000). *The building blocks of experience: An early framework for interaction designers*. Paper presented at the the Conference on Designing Interactive Systems: Processes, Practices, Methods, and Techniques, New York.

Gaver, W., Dunne, T., & Pacenti, E. (1999). Design: Cultural probes. *Interactions, 6*(1), 21–29.

Gibson, J. J. (1979). *The ecological approach to visual perception*. New York: Houghton-Mifflin.

Hassenzahl, M. (2004). The interplay of beauty, goodness, and usability in interactive products. *Human-Computer Interactions, 19*, 319–349.

Hassenzahl, M., & Tractinsky, N. (2006). User experience—A research agenda. *Behaviour and Information Technology, 25*(2), 91–97.

Husserl, E. (1931). *Ideas: General introduction to pure phenomenology*. London: George Allen & Unwin Ltd.

ISO-9241-11. (1998). Guidance on usability.

Jääskö, V., & Mattelmäki, T. (2003). *Observing and Probing*. Paper presented at the Proceedings of the 2003 International Conference on Designing Pleasurable Products and Interfaces, Pittsburgh.

Johnson-Laird, P. N. (1988). How is meaning mentally represented? In U. Eco, M. Santambrogio, & P. Violi (Eds.), *Meaning and mental representations*. Indianapolis: Indiana University Press.

Jordan, P. W. (1999). *Designing pleasurable products: An introduction to the new human factors*. London: Taylor & Francis.

Kahneman, D. (1999). Objective happiness. In D. Kahneman, E. Diener, & N. Schwartz (Eds.), *Well-being: The foundations of hedonic psychology* (pp. 3–25). New York: Russell Sage Foundation.

Kahneman, D., Diener, E., & Schwartz, N. (1999). *Well-being: The foundations of hedonic psychology*. New York: Russell Sage Foundation.

Kaplan, R., & Kaplan, S. (1989). *The experience of nature: A psychological perspective*. New York: Cambridge University Press.

Kelly, G. A. (1955). *The psychology of personal constructs, volume one: Theory and personality* (1991 ed. Vol. 1). London: Routledge.

Kelly, G. A. (2003). A brief introduction to personal construct theory. In F. Fransella (Ed.), *International handbook of personal construct psychology*. Chichester: Wiley.

Kuniavsky, M. (2003). *Observing the user experience: A practitioner's guide to user research.* San Francisco: Morgan Kaufman.

Lakoff, G. (1987). *Women, fire, and dangerous things.* Chicago: University of Chicago Press.

Lidwell, W., Holden, K., & Butler, J. (2003). *Universal principles of design.* Beverly: Rockport.

Light, A. (2006). Adding method to meaning: a technique for exploring people's experience with technology. *Behaviour & Information Technology, 25*(2), 175–187.

Maslow, A. H. (1987). *Motivation and personality* (Vol. 3). New York: HarperCollins.

McCarthy, J., & Wright, P. C. (2003). Technology as experience (special issue). *Special Issue of Interactions Magazine: More Funology, 9,* 42–43.

McCarthy, J., & Wright, P. C. (2004). *Technology as experience.* Cambridge: MIT Press.

McCarthy, J., Wright, P. C., & Meekison, L. (2005). A practitioner-centred assessment of a user-experience framework. *International Journal of Technology and Human Interaction, 1*(2), 1–23.

Mehrabian, A., & Russell, J. A. (1974). *An approach to environmental psychology.* Cambridge: MIT Press.

Mynatt, C. R., Doherty, M. E., & Tweney, R. D. (1977). Confirmation bias in a simulated research environment: An experimental study of scientific inference. *Quarterly Journal of Experimental Psychology, 29*(1), 85–95.

Norman, D. A. (1990). *The design of everyday things.* New York: Basic Books.

Norman, D. A. (2003). *Emotional design: Why we love (or hate) everyday things.* New York: Basic Books.

Orme, J. E. (1969). *Time, experience and behaviour.* London: Iliffe Books.

Osgood, C. E., Suci, G. J., & Tannenbaum, P. H. (1957). *The measurement of meaning.* Urbana: Illinois University Press.

Pine, J. B., & Gilmore, J. H. (1999). *The experience economy.* Boston: Harvard Business School Press.

Richins, M. L. (1994). Valuing things: The public and private meanings of possessions. *Journal of Consumer Research, 21*(3), 504–521.

Seligman, M. E. P., & Csikszentmihalyi, M. (2000). Positive psychology: An introduction. *American Psychologist, 55,* 5–14.

Tiger, L. (1992). *The pursuit of pleasure.* Boston: Little, Brown & Company.

Yerkes, R. M., & Dodson, J. D. (1908). The relation of strength of stimulus to rapidity of habit-formation. *Journal of Comparative Neurology and Psychology, 18*(459), 482.

Zajonc, R. B. (1980). Feeling & thinking: preferences need no inferences. *American Psychologist, 35*(2), 151–175.

Zakay, D., & Block, R. A. (1997). Temporal cognition. *Current Directions in Psychological Science, 6,* 12–16.

Chapter 3
Measuring Experience

Abstract Following on from the previous theoretical discussion, this chapter critiques several studies that are relevant to UX in terms of psychological constructs. Particular points of interest are meaningful relationships, self-identity, as well as the value and meaning in objects. Also of interest here are concepts such as novelty, coherence, complexity, habituation and preference; parallels are drawn with principles derived from environmental psychology where technology is viewed as a 'scene'. In addition, aesthetics are explored closely with reference to several studies that identify a strong link between aesthetics and usability. The dynamics of UX are also examined in detail with respect to several different timescales: minutes, hours, days, months, and years. Finally, a number of research methods are introduced which are useful for identifying key constructs and evaluative elements of UX. They include experience sampling, content analysis, grounded theory, and a number of techniques with a strong phenomenological basis derived from Kelly's Personal Construct Theory (PCT), including the Repertory Grid Test (RGT) and Multiple Sorting Procedure (MSP).

Keywords Human–computer interaction (HCI) • Mobile device usability • Multiple sorting procedure (MSP) • Personal Construct Theory (PCT) • Phenomenology • Sense making • User experience (UX) • User experience dynamics • UX-scale • Aesthetics • Time • Meaning

As discussed in the previous chapter, the construction process is seen as the 'glue' to experience, where constructs are the basic 'components' of the sense-making processes. People use these constructs to differentiate between various stimuli and events, and are therefore a primary ingredient in how users make meaning. The constructs and the meanings that are embedded in the way users relate to objects, are constantly revised and overturned as part of the overall experience.

A. al-Azzawi, *Experience with Technology*, SpringerBriefs in Computer Science, 31
DOI: 10.1007/978-1-4471-5397-9_3, © The Author(s) 2014

There is a plethora of research and design methods available for practitioners who are interested in researching people's experience with technology (Kumar 2013). However, this chapter is specifically concerned with discussing methods and empirical findings from studies that explore the relationships and meanings that people attribute to objects, and the role that constructs play in this regard. Also, as time is fundamental to experience, this chapter will also be used to review empirical studies on how people's judgement and meanings change over time, both in the short and long-term.

3.1 Making Sense of Experience

As already shown, sense-making is a fundamental aspect of experience. Also, sense-making and meaning-making maybe seen as synonymous. However, of the different ways of defining meaning, it is not the *denotative* meaning that is important here, rather it is the *connotative* meaning that provides inference about evaluative and emotional aspects of technology. Therefore, to follow the constructive aspects of user experience in ICE, the kind of meaning that is important in this analysis is *symbolic meaning*. A symbol (e.g. an event or object) is a result of "a cognitive process whereby an object acquires connotation beyond its instrumental use" (Lang 1988, p. 13). Therefore, objects and technological artifacts themselves have no inherent meaning, and may be regarded as stimuli or 'signs'. In this way, the meaning of an MP3 player is not just that 'it is a device that plays music', but may also be 'a fun thing to have when travelling', or 'a way of defining social status', or a mixture of the above, depending on context. Also, even such mundane objective qualities like the shape, colour, and size may connote some meaning, based on direct or indirect past experiences. They can act as simple associative markers, even though the associations themselves are not the meanings. In fact, software developers rely on standardising shapes of elements in an interface (e.g. design patterns), in order to use them as signs or symbols, as part of an orchestrated effort in semiotics. Ultimately, these signs get used to convey messages about functionality within the user interface (Souza 2005). The domain of such engineered signs can extend outside the computer, and into the environment. For example, just by mere sight of a 'WiFi' logo in a café, an user may understand the location to be one of being able to connect with friends and family while on holiday, and the café may become a meaningful place of high emotional value. In this example, the technology becomes a mediator to the meaning of the valued relationships. This meaning is therefore *extrinsic*, i.e. it is not the WiFi that is important, but the relationship (see McCarthy and Wright 2004, p. 114). The *intrinsic* meaning on the other hand is the meaning that is associated with the act itself, i.e. connecting to the Internet, and perhaps enjoying or hating the conuration process. The relationship between such signs, artifacts and the user are important and there have been many suggestions that such relationships are at the centre of UX [e.g. Forlizzi and Ford (2000)].

3.1.1 Meaning and Value in Things

Csikszentmihalyi and Rochberg-Halton (1981) conducted a major study regarding "the meaning of things". They interviewed members of 82 families (315 participants) in the Chicago Metropolitan area, where they explored how people related to special objects in their home. They defined a thing as "any bit of information that has a recognisable identity in consciousness" (Csikszentmihalyi and Rochberg-Halton 1981, p. 14). This was one of many studies that highlighted the idea that value is not in the artifact itself, but in the meaning that is attributed to it. Of the 1,694 'things' identified in the homes, there were 41 categories, e.g. *clothes, sculpture, tools, stereo, musical instruments,* and *pets*. They suggested that these objects can "communicate the continuity of one's experiences, relationships, and values" (Csikszentmihalyi and Rochberg-Halton 1981, p. 224). They also showed that such value is derived from repeated person-object interactions with a possession (Csikszentmihalyi and Rochberg-Halton 1981, p. 173). However, they found that the objects "are valued because of social meanings they embody, such as ties to kin, or effort or money spent. They classified the meanings that these objects had into 37 types, e.g. *personal values, style, utilitarian, the past, experiences, kin* and *self*. Therefore, the "objective qualities only serve the purpose of recognition" (Csikszentmihalyi and Rochberg-Halton 1981, p. 180), and these artifacts can become simply the elements that hold experiences together.

Other empirical studies have been undertaken from the point of view of 'possessions' and their perceived value (Prentice 1987; Richins 1994). In particular, Richins (1994) explored the sources of meaning in these relationships, and undertook three studies with well-educated participants from middle- to upper-middle social classes. She suggested that there were two types of meaning: *public* and *private* meaning. These two types are created and influenced by different mechanisms. Public meanings tend to be the result of socialisation factors such as advertising that promote associations with social groups and certain values, as well as participation in shared environments and activities. These meanings can be derived without actual contact with the consumer products, and may be exchanged via narratives. Private meanings, on the other hand, are strongly linked to actual experiences that a person may have with a particular artifact, and these meanings tend to be idiosyncratic. Richins also pointed out that private meanings are more likely to emerge from products that allow for greater personalisation or range of activities. In this respect, an MP3 player that allows for personal selection of music to be played (or other personal data, e.g. photos), has greater potential for personal meaning than a TV that may have limited scope for customisation.

In Richin's (1994) study, participants were given cards that represented possessions, and were asked to "sort into piles the possessions that might be valued for similar reasons", into any number of piles. These data were analysed using Multidimensional Scaling (MDS), which yielded three dimensions to meanings: *Instrumental-Symbolic, Ordinary-Prestige,* and *Necessity-Recreational*. The first dimension of *instrumental-symbolic* meaning showed items such as 'TV' and

'CD player' on the instrumental end, and 'photos' and 'trophies' on the symbolic end. The dimension of *ordinary-prestige* showed 'electric shaver' and 'tools' on the ordinary end, while the prestige end showed items such as a 'mink coat' and 'Mercedes car'. The third dimension of *necessity-recreational* included 'car' and 'house' on the necessary end, while items such as 'exercise bike' and 'gun collection' were on the recreational end.

Richins suggested that "a possession's public and private meanings are what give it value" (Richins 1994, p. 506). Through content analysis of her interview data, she found that a possession is valued for many reasons. People tended to value possessions for *utilitarian* reasons, as well as *enjoyment* and *financial* aspects. They also valued possessions for what they gave them in terms of *self-identity*, including enhancement to their *physical image*. People also valued possessions for contributing to *interpersonal ties*, e.g. a gift from a friend. The issue of self-identity was also apparent in several studies of such relationships that were carried out by Dittmar (1992). One of her conclusions was that consumers believe that "to have is to be", i.e. their purchase helps them take-on the identity they want be. For example, an MP3 player may be marketed via the image of a sporty and energetic young person, and a consumer may want to buy that item so that they can 'be' the person in the advert. The implication is that values of 'sporty', 'energetic' and 'young' are high values to the target consumer.

3.1.2 Meaningful Relationships

These values and meanings were also observed in other studies. Battarbee and Mattelmäki (2002) collected 113 stories and essays from participants ranging from children to elderly people who expressed their meaningful relationships with products. The relationships were classified into three categories: *meaningful tool*, *meaningful association*, and *living object*. The 'meaningful tool' refers to objects that allow a person to perform a task that is meaningful to them and helps them realise one or more values. The tool itself is not meaningful, and can therefore be replaced by another tool if need be. For example a public telephone can be used to keep in touch with a friend, and any public telephone will do the job. This is also an example of intrinsic meaning, where the task itself is the meaningful part. This category essentially includes the instrumental values outlined above. The meaningful association category refers to a direct link between a particular experience and that object, for example a gift for a special occasion or ceremony. In this case, the associations and memories may be connected to the event or place, and perhaps the identity that was cultivated during the special occasion. This is an example of the symbolic aspects of the meaning dimensions suggested by Richins (1994). The living object category is concerned with objects that take a life of their own. For example, a person may see a particular artifact (e.g. a mobile phone) as something that has been with them a long time and has "endured long journeys through thick and thin". In such a relationship, a person may be reluctant to upgrade to newer technology, and may see more value in keeping the object itself for its meaning.

However, other researchers suggested that there were 'deeper' meanings to such relationships between person and object. In a very large qualitative study across the United States that was designed to explore people's relationships with objects, 24 researchers collected 4,000 still photographs (that are meaningful to the participants), and 140 interview video recordings with the participants (15–18 min each). In analysing the data for meanings that consumers attribute to possessions, Wallendorf et al. (1988), found four themes of *deep meaning*. The first was that possessions extended the *sense of self*, as shown above and by other research (Belk 1988). The second that they found is similar to the 'living object' above, however, they specifically referred to it as *anthropomorphism*, where the owner is treating an object as a human, as well as *totemism*, where the person is getting 'strength' from an object. However, an interesting category of deep meaning was *fetishism*. In this they meant that a person may give extreme attention or devotion to a class of possessions, to the extent that they may exhibit addictive or compulsive behaviour. The fourth category of deep meaning was *sacred*. This is more than fetishism, it is almost a reverence (in a secular fashion), where objects are seen as "mystical, powerful and deserving of reverential behaviour" (Belk 1988, p. 529).

3.1.3 Evaluative Responses

Although people respond to their own evaluation of their constructions of meaning and the relationship to their possessions, they also respond to environmental stimuli in various ways. A basic manifestation of evaluation is orientation: "processes that focus, direct, or sensitize receptor organs and thus have an unmistakable exploratory function" (Berlyne 1960, p. 95), also referred to as the "what-is-it?" reflex by Pavlov, and are seen as strong evaluative responses, whereas arousal is a scale related to the level of attention, ranging from sleep or coma, to frantic excitement (Berlyne 1960, p. 48). In the context of technology, Berlyne's (1960, p. 96) orientation response could be the result of several factors, e.g. colour, indicating stimulus, novelty, surprisingness and complexity. In other words, if the colour or visual complexity of some device is so deviant from the norm, it could cause an orientation response. Another evaluative response is affect, and according to Norman (2003, p. 20), "affect is an evaluative system, whereas cognition is a system for interpretation and understanding", which will eventually lead to an approach-avoidance response. This response can either be preceded by cognitive activity that distils all available data into meaning (Mandler 1990), or a person may have an evaluative response that produces an affective response without any cognitive activity (Zajonc 1980). Affect is seen here as an evaluative component of various environmental stimuli. Importantly, there is no directionality implied; cognition and affect have been shown to influence each other (Castro et al. 1998; Rholes et al. 1987), including the manifestation as anxiety towards technology (Chua et al. 1999). Affect has also been shown to have a modulating influence on recall and cognition (Isen 1990). Also, first impression evaluations have been shown to have a lasting effect on preference. Lindgaard et al. (2006) undertook a study which showed that the preference towards web sites was cemented in the first 50 ms of exposure, was largely similar to the preference after several minutes of exposure and use (Lindgaard et al. 2006). Such evaluations are too quick to be reflective or interpretive in nature, however, they ultimately lead to preferences.

Preference has also been seen as a form of evaluation, and the 'discrepancy hypothesis' has been proposed as a way of explaining some preferences. This hypothesis suggests that people's preferences are maximised when the stimulus is not at the adaptation level (i.e. typical), but at some different level. In other words, the most preferred stimulus is different to what is perceived as typical (McClelland et al. 1953; Mehrabian and Russell 1974, p. 105). The degree of typicality of a stimulus has been the subject of study for many researchers, where some models propose that a person holds a schema of what is 'typical' for a stimulus category and is constantly making comparisons with such representations (Purcell 1986; Purcell and Nasar 1992). This model of 'similarities and differences' has been useful in exploring theory behind preference responses. Equally, the notion of 'familiarity' is also relevant here, where studies have shown 'typicality' and 'familiarity' influencing 'interest' and 'preference' and are related to how far away from 'typical' a stimulus may be.

Also related to typicality, novelty has been the subject of extensive study. According to Berlyne (1960, p. 19), novelty can be seen in several different ways: *short-term*, *long-term*, *complete-absolute*, and *relative* novelty. Short-term novelty is related to stimuli that have occurred in the past, but not recently. Long-term novelty relates to stimuli with longer absence, e.g. days or months. Complete and absolute novelty is concerned with stimuli that have never occurred. Relative novelty, on the other hand, is one that has some elements about the experience that are completely new, and others that are familiar. These types of novelty may occur in varying degrees when experiencing technology using a familiar computer system with a new pointing device may elicit a response of 'relative novelty', whereas using a computer system that a person has not used for several months may elicit a response of 'long-term novelty'.

Also related to novelty, it is important to note the 'habituation' phenomenon, which plays an important role in experience. This is where an effect may be measurable with certain frequency of exposure of stimuli, but then has a different response when varying the duration and frequency of exposure. This can also manifest itself in a 'sensitisation' effect. The effects of sensitisation and habituation have been shown to be separate processes which are part of a *dual process theory* (Groves and Thompson 1970). These issues relate to experience with technology because consumers of technology get sensitised to functionality. Anecdotally, this can be seen when users no longer respond to the 'wow factor' of a new technology, and grow to expect it from subsequent releases of updated

Table 3.1 The preference matrix described by Kaplan and Kaplan (1989, p. 53)

	Understanding	Exploration
Immediate	Coherence	Complexity
Inferred, predicted	Legibility	Mystery

technology. This effect may be combined with manufacturers competing with each other by taking part in this race for functionality, size and quality, etc.

Preference has also been explored from the point of view of 'information'. In their investigation of the experience of nature, Kaplan and Kaplan (1989), have used the theme of information processing to understand preference with regards to environmental psychology. Although they used this approach with respect to a 'natural scene', this approach is applied here with respect to technology as 'a scene', i.e. 'technology as environment.' They also adopted a holistic approach to their study, rather than the reductive experiments used in the experimental aesthetics methods (e.g. Berlyne 1974). This was argued to give more ecological validity to their findings.

Over the course of several empirical studies, Kaplan and Kaplan (1989, p. 57) found that people mostly preferred scenes that showed *mystery* (Table 3.1), where there was hidden or partial information that invited exploration. Mystery is used here to denote something related to being drawn-into a scene by way of some promise that encourages a viewer to enter and venture. Kaplan and Kaplan suggest that in order for mystery to be present "there must be a promise of further information if one could walk deeper into the scene" (Kaplan and Kaplan 1989, p. 56). Mystery is described as a flowing experience, where a viewer or user may be moving from one aspect of a scene to another in a smooth fashion. This is contrasted with surprise, according to Kaplan and Kaplan, where there is a stopping sensation, and a sense of unknown, where further exploration may or may not be possible. In the context of technology, this may translate to a preference for devices that are well understood conceptually, yet allow the user to explore other, hidden aspects of the functionality of the device. Conversely, users may dislike a device that is conceptually complex or incoherent, where even reading the manual leaves them still confused.

However, scenes with well maintained and ordered paths scored high on *legibility* measures. The concept of 'legibility' was first introduced by Lynch (1960) in the context of a 'city scene'. This notion refers to the extent that a viewer is able to understand a scene, e.g. a city, by way of having a mental map. The more a viewer is able to find their way around a city and find their way back, the more legible a city is said to be. This same concept may be applied to technology. The more an user is able to understand their way around the use of a device or a technological setting, the more legible the technological 'scene' is. In this context, legibility would have an influence on preference in a technological setting. Kaplan and Kaplan define coherence as "a sense of order … anything that helps organize the patterns of brightness, size and texture in the scene into a few major units" (Kaplan and Kaplan 1989, p. 50). They also relate coherence to the concept of 'legibility', however, a lack of coherence may sometimes not be a negative issue, but may

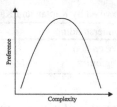

Fig. **3.1** Relationship of preference and complexity (Walker 1973, p. 73)

elicit a sense of exploration, or a type of curiosity. For example if a person does not understand the stimulus, and is sufficiently motivated, or may see some potential of fun, then the user may want to explore further. Also, Kaplan and Kaplan argued that having an explorative aspect to a scene is directly proportional to preference because of the natural tendency for humans to explore and build on previous knowledge (Kaplan and Kaplan 1989, p. 50). Scenes exhibiting high complexity and low coherence scored low preferences.

Table 3.1 also refers to visual complexity, which is related to the number of visual elements and the intricacy of the scene "how much is going on" (Kaplan and Kaplan 1989, p. 53). The relationship between preference and complexity was also found to follow an inverted 'U' function, where it has been found to have a peak at moderate complexity (Walker 1973; Yerkes and Dodson 1908) (Fig. 3.1). This is also similar to the balance shown between complexity (overwhelm) and simplicity (boredom), described by the concept of 'flow' or optimal-experience (Csikszentmihalyi 1990).

However, conceptual complexity is a matter of how a person understands the scene, and how coherent it is for them. The notion of coherence is used here to describe the degree of organisation of the scene. Aspects of the scene that can enhance coherence are where elements are organised in groups that make sense, or in order of size, function, context etc. Table 3.2 shows how coherence and complexity may be related. It is important to note that a scene can be complex as well as coherent and that these two properties are not polar opposites of a continuum.

3.1.4 Aesthetics and the Joy of Use

As well as the aspects discussed above, many studies have shown that aesthetics are also involved in affective responses, and play an important role in user experience and preference (Hartman et al. 2008; Hassenzahl 2004b; Lindgaard and

Table **3.2** The relationship between coherence and complexity (Kaplan and Kaplan 1989, p. 54)

	Complexity	
Coherence	Low	High
Low	Not much there	Visually messy
High	Clear and simple	Rich and organised

Dudek 2002; Tractinsky et al. 2000). However, there have been many attempts at classifying aesthetic responses. One way of distinguishing between categories of aesthetics is to divide them into three types: *sensory*, *formal* and *symbolic* (Lang 1988, p. 11). Sensory aesthetics refer to sensations that give pleasure through the arousal of the senses, e.g. odour, and sound. According to the 'New Experimental Aesthetics' discipline (Berlyne 1974), formal aesthetics are related to aspects such as shape, complexity, and rhythm. These stimuli are said to induce physiological responses, e.g. the response to the golden ratio rectangle (Russell 2000). Symbolic aesthetics, on the other hand, are the connotative and associational aspects of a stimulus.

Of the three types of aesthetics outlined above, the latter two, formal and symbolic, have also been suggested as two separate dimensions of aesthetics by Lavie and Tractinsky (2004). They suggested that aesthetics could be classified into two types: *classical aesthetics* and *expressive aesthetics*. They derived this taxonomy by undertaking four studies to explore the aesthetics of web sites, and using exploratory factor analysis methods to find dimensions of aesthetics. Classical aesthetics related to order and clarity of design, and perhaps the tendency to exhibit such properties as symmetry. Conversely, expressive aesthetics related to novelty and departure from typicality by the designer, and were more related to transient effects such as fashion, as well as symbolic aspects. The above classifications are somewhat similar to the suggestion that artifacts, in general, should be assessed according to *aesthetics, instrumentality*, and *symbolism* (Rafaeli and Vilnai-Yavetz 2004).

Interestingly, there is evidence that the non-instrumental aspects of objects, such as aesthetics and symbolism, may influence instrumental aspects such as usability (Kurosu and Kashimura 1995). Usability is defined here as "the extent to which a product can be used by specified users to achieve specified goals with *effectiveness*, *efficiency* and *satisfaction* in a specified context of use" (ISO-9241-11 1998). Tractinsky et al. claimed that "what is beautiful is usable" (Tractinsky et al. 2000). They made their claim after they tested the performance of ATM cash machines with different interfaces; well-presented, attractive ones, and badly presented, ugly ones. The study was initially designed to test the prospect that such effects are culturally related, but their results did not confirm this hypothesis. The results confirmed that such effects are not culturally related, and, even though the underlying system was exactly the same (between well presented and badly presented interfaces), they found that users faced fewer usability problems with well-presented interfaces. They concluded that the reason was the psychological state of the user was more favourable when faced with a well-presented interface, and the user is more likely to be more forgiving of little annoyances, and find a way through usability problems. This phenomenon may also be related to the 'halo effect', where one dominant attribute affects the perception of the whole (Asch 1946; Thorndike 1920). In other words, an attribute of a stimulus (e.g. colour), may be such a strong stimulus that it overrides other attributes. This effect was also noticed by Dion et al. who concluded that "what is beautiful is good" (Dion et al. 1972). In other words, things seem more usable if they look good or if they are in the presence of other things that make the user feel good.

The effect of aesthetics on use was also explored by Hassenzahl et al. (2002). In a study of pre- and post-use of web sites, ratings of *pragmatic quality* were seen to be dependent on the task given to participants. If the participants were given the device to 'play with' only, then pragmatic quality was not affected by use. However, if the participants were asked to perform a task, then the results showed a strong correlation between *pragmatic quality* and *appeal*. However, in a later study, Hassenzahl (2004b) proposed a model based on the hypothesis that *usability* influences *goodness*. He investigated the interplay between *usability*, *beauty* and *goodness*. Goodness was defined as an aspect that is related to *hedonic identification*, *pragmatic values*, and *mental effort*. The study was conducted using virtual MP3 players (i.e. software based, running on a PC), where the functional aspects were kept constant, while varying the visual and layout aspects using a 'skin'. Each participant was given the same four skins that were chosen as extremes of 'ugly' and 'beautiful' by a previous group of participants.

Using a questionnaire, based on one developed in separate studies (Hassenzahl 2001; Hassenzahl et al. 2003), the participants rated the skins before using the software (Hassenzahl 2004b), and then asked to rate their experience using the same questionnaire, with an emphasis on change, i.e. asking them to focus on the change in their rating, if any. Although, Hassenzahl suggested that this "should reduce participants' implicit need for a consistent rating" (Hassenzahl 2004b, p. 336), such 'leading' instruction (asking about "change" draws attention to it, even if it was not salient) could be seen to undermine the validity of the data. Nonetheless, results showed that hedonic attributes and beauty aspects were stable over time, whereas 'perceived usability' was influenced by experience, indicated by increased mental effort.

In contradiction to the abovementioned ATM study (Tractinsky et al. 2000), Hassenzahl's study did not find any association between the actual experience of usability and beauty (as an evaluative construct). In fact, the data suggested that 'goodness', as an evaluative construct, influenced the overall evaluation of an experience with technology, not beauty. This contradiction seeded a debate on the nature of beauty in HCI (Norman 2004), where Frohlich (2004) resisted Hassenzahl's use of the term, and argued that beauty is a "rare and discrete response by users to something they see in these products", and not something to be measured as a continuous property, echoing Kant's assertion that "beauty is in the eye of the beholder". Hassenzahl defended his position by explaining that he intended to measure the "*content* of beauty" (Hassenzahl 2004a, p. 379). By this he meant the attributes of an object that people see (physical or otherwise), and then give it value. These attributes ultimately must have a physical manifestation that is objective, such as colour, shape or brand logo. Hence, it follows that these attributes can therefore be measured.

In contrast to the quantitative work described above, some qualitative research has also been undertaken regarding people's experience with digital artifacts. One interesting project used three case studies of three participants using Smartphones to investigate the themes of experience with such interactive devices (Swallow et al. 2005). The researchers used a *grounded theory* method to analyse qualitative interview and diary data of participants' accounts of their experiences over a three-week period. The result of the study suggested four themes underlying people's experience with such devices: *identity, sociability, security* and *organisation*. As might be expected, identity relates to the aspects of the experience that are linked to the persons sense of their own identity that may be exhibited through the use of technology. Sociability refers to the communicative aspect, and thereby the relationships that underlie the use of such devices. The security aspect was primarily related to the confidential data stored on the device, as well as the monetary value attached to the Smartphone.

In order to arrive at a richer set of evaluations, (Vyas and Veer 2006) chose to combine several approaches and techniques to measure user experience. They carried out an in-depth qualitative study to evaluate participants' experience with an Internet-based TV product (IPTV). In their study, eleven participants took part in a lab-based three-phase procedure. The first phase included the *pre-experience* open interview, and the second phase was the task-based and *interactive stage*. The final phase was the *post-experience* stage, where the participants were asked to give their overall impression and experience with the interactive device. The researchers took note of the constructive nature of experience, and used constructs derived from the literature in order to help participants articulate their experience. They used constructs such as *simple, familiar, original, exciting* etc. The pre-experience interviews allowed the participants to reflect on other interactive technologies, and their everyday TV watching experience, including expectations from brands and expectations of functionality from new upcoming technologies. This stage of the data collection allowed the researchers access to the constructions and anticipations of the participants. The post-experience data also show participants reflecting on their expectations for the functionalities as well as the brand, and how they were met (or not). This is an example of Kelly's re-construing by 'man the scientist', where the participants were making sense of their recent experience, in the light of new 'evidence', and assimilating new understandings, and thereby creating new experiences.

Vyas and Veer (2006) concluded that being able to provide rich evaluations of users' own interpretations, using the users' own words, was a key factor in being able to give "justice to the 'actual', 'lived' experiences of the users". The study also underlined the influence of the constructive and symbolic aspects of the product to towards the overall experience. The authors suggested that the "professional look and feel of this system" added to the perceived quality of the system, as far as the participants saw it. However, they also added that "the main functionalities, interaction mechanisms and usability" also influenced the users' positive experience (Vyas and Veer 2006, p. 144). In other words, the visual 'signs', e.g. colour, styling, typography etc., as well as the expectations from the brand, and of course, the setting of the actual interview of the study in the laboratory, will have played a part in the whole experience.

McCarthy and Wright (2004) undertook a study which minimises possible confounds introduced by the artificial settings described above. They carried out a case study to explore the prosaic experience of shopping on an ecommerce web site (McCarthy and Wright 2004, p. 131). Their study highlighted the experience of a buyer of wine on the Virgin Wines web site, and they showed how the sense-making framework they developed, as well as the threads of experience (discussed earlier), can be used to "see the felt life" (McCarthy and Wright 2004, p. 131). There were several examples of how the emotions felt by the user were under-going transformation, e.g. from surprise, to annoyance, to curiosity, when going through the first impressions with the web site itself. Also, there were several examples of understandings and past experiences of the Virgin brand, and with the wine culture, which highlight the expectations through the whole experience.

McCarthy and Wright also emphasised the dynamic aspects of the case study, where not only emotions, but meanings were shifting from "difficulty, anxiety and hardship at the time, becomes heroic adventure in the retelling" (McCarthy and Wright 2004, p. 142). Therefore, meanings can change, not only at the time, but at the recounting stage. These meanings, however, were not related to 'one world' for the user. The analysis showed that buying wine on the Internet can become a complex array of interlinked 'worlds': "the world of wine buying, the world of online shopping, and the world of technology" (McCarthy and Wright 2004, p. 143). Also, the way the user was making sense of this experience also included the 'sociality' of the experience: "sense making is always at the boundary of self and other". In other words, the user must be aware of the 'other' in order for the experience to make sense (also seen in Swallow et al. 2005). However, there was also an illustration of the 'unfinalisability' of the experiences, and the experience as a whole, i.e. experience is never final. Just as with the example of the shifts in meaning within the experience, McCarthy and Wright show how the ever-moving boundaries are illustrated by examples such as early delays in the web site that are later re-construed as crashes that were narrowly avoided (McCarthy and Wright 2004, p. 144). For McCarthy and Wright, the fact that they were able to find examples of the processes described by their framework is evidence that the concepts they described in the sense making and threads of experience are valu-able ways of "seeing experience" as it unfolds.

3.1.5 Time is Everything

As shown in the previous chapter, experience and time are inextricably linked, and therefore it is not possible to have experience without time. This assertion cre-ates a problem when referring to the idea of 'dynamics' of experience, because 'dynamics' means changes, and to 'experience' is to 'feel the changes'. This cir-cular definition is highlighting a tautology in the use of this term. Therefore, in order to move forward without getting stuck in circular arguments, 'dynamics' will be defined as the changes between experiences, such that each experience is the sum integral of a range of experiences. In other words, there is a perceived change between experience-1 and experience-2.

As discussed so far, to measure experience is to measure meaning-making and value perception, because they are directly correlated. Further, the meanings that people attribute to events and artifacts, change on a continual basis. Such shifts in meaning can occur for many reasons, and one such reason is conflict between public and private meanings. According to Richins (1994) there are three possible sources for conflict or incongruence in meanings held by a person: "When a possession is first acquired, its public and private meanings may be reasonably consistent; but over time, private meanings are likely to shift because of personal experiences with the object" (Richins 1994, p. 518). These shifts in meaning can be the reasons for the dissolution of relationships between people and artifacts. Three different areas of potential conflict are: when a previously valued possession is degraded by social influences, or becomes technologically obsolete. Another area of conflict is when public meaning and perception of an object is at odds with self-image, and therefore private meaning. And finally, conflict can occur when shared meaning is not negotiated successfully, and members of a sub-group do not share private meaning. This causes constant tension, for example when family members have different meanings for the same object. In the above examples, these shifts in meaning can occur *after* a consumer acquires the possession, and is therefore faced with the incongruence of owning or using something, they are now uncomfortable with.

There have been, however, only a few studies that have had an explicit interest in exploring the dynamics of user experience. In particular, there have been surprisingly few studies addressing the very early stages of micro-dynamics, e.g. the study showing how as little as 50 ms of exposure to web sites will have an enduring effect on people's judgments of preference (Lindgaard et al. 2006). General usability studies usually take a timescale of the order of minutes. However, for *micro-dynamics* of the order of a few minutes, where aspects of experience are measured longitudinally before *and* after interaction, there is a distinct scarcity. A particularly noteworthy study which was discussed earlier, was Hassenzahl's software-based MP3 player study (Hassenzahl 2004b), and two other studies using simulated MP3 players on a touch-screen (Minge 2008; Thüring and Mahlke 2007).

For physical media devices (not software based), one study measured people's rating of four physical MP3 players after interaction, where the different MP3 players "differed in … various design aspects" (Mahlke 2006, p. 4). The study was designed to investigate the influence of instrumental and non-instrumental aspects of the devices upon overall judgements. Thirty participants were given each MP3 player separately (all of the same brand), in order to use it for set tasks, and then given a rating questionnaire to assess qualities such as usefulness, ease of use, goodness, and aesthetics. The questionnaire was a mixture of the ratings used in the Hassenzahl's study (2004b), as well as other ones added to account for Jordan's pleasure distinctions (1999), and classical and expressive aesthetics (Lavie and Tractinsky 2004). Mahlke demonstrated that for physical devices too, non-instrumental qualities do indeed have a role to play in overall judgement, to confirm the earlier results with software MP3 players (Hassenzahl 2004b). These results were also confirmed later using simulated MP3 players displayed on a touch-screen (Thüring and Mahlke 2007). In that study, researchers asked participants to rate aesthetics aspects before interaction, and then usability aspects after interaction only. Their results indicated that aesthetics showed a trend of influence on perceived usability.

In order to measure the changes in judgements, pre- and post-interaction, Minge (2008) used software-based MP3 players. The audio players were conured in such a way to enable independent changes in layout, and presentation, as well as changes in menu conuration (to manipulate usability). Sixty participants were asked to rate two audio players at three time points: pre-interaction, after 2 min of free-use, and after 15 min of task based use. Minge's results confirmed earlier studies showing a correlation between attractiveness and usability, where attractiveness tended to overshadow perceived usability, before use. Importantly though, the overshadowing was not maintained after the second time point. In other words, once the participants had rated the player as low in usability, attractiveness had no influence over the rating at the last time point.

For *meso-dynamics* (days to weeks) Mendoza and Novick (2005) measured people's experience with web sites over an eight-week period, showing a decline in levels of frustration with time, where users were more inclined to work through problems. Karapanos et al. (2009) also carried out a longitudinal study where they measured users' judgments of their own experience during the week prior to their purchase of physical artifacts (mobile phones), and then on-going for four weeks after the purchase date. From 482 recorded narratives, the data were analysed using content analysis for recurring themes. The data yielded several themes relating to user experience dynamics. The researchers then used these themes to propose a model of the "temporality of experience". The model proposed anticipation and expectations to be central themes, while *familiarity*, *functional dependency* and *emotional attachments* to be "forces" that motivate the user across the three main phases of use: *orientation*, *incorporation*, and *identification* (based on a model proposed by Silverstone and Haddon 1996). Orientation relates to "initial experiences" e.g. excitements or frustrations, while incorporation refers to the attribution of meaning to the object, and incorporating it into daily life. Identification is the process of taking on the object as part of the self-identity. The quantitative data showed that the number of reported experiences of stimulation and learnability declined during the orientation phase in the weeks after purchase, while usefulness and usability show no discernable trend during the next phase, which is the incorporation phase (for both satisfying and dissatisfying experiences). Interestingly, there were no reported experiences of a dissatisfying nature during the final phase, the identification phase, for both personal and social identification. This suggests that all the participants identified positively with the device as time passed, which is consistent with the view that the meaning of the object "becomes realized in the activity of interaction" (Csikszentmihalyi and Rochberg-Halton 1981, p. 174), therefore, as interaction takes place, meaning is being made, and is susceptible to change. These data give clues towards stable versus volatile constructs, suggesting that relational constructs (e.g. social identification) are more stable, than usability or stimulation constructs (e.g. novelty).

A study by von Wilamowitz-Moellendorff et al. (2006) focused on the *macro-dynamic* (several weeks or more) experiences of mobile phone users. The participants were chosen as 'experts', i.e. they have used their own phone for 1–2 years. The participants were interviewed and asked to rate their experiences retrospectively, i.e. thinking of how their felt about their phones in the past 1–2 years, and make judgements based on the parameters in Hassenzahl's study (2004b): *utility*, *usability*, *stimulation*, *beauty* and *identity*. However, the reliability of such data where participant were asked to recall their past-experiences may not be as good as data based on current experience. The issue of unfinalisability of meaning and experience has already been raised earlier (McCarthy and Wright 2004), and it also applies in this case too. In other words, a person recalling a past experience, is recalling it in their current way of attributing meaning, and may not recall it in the way they experienced it at the time, only the way it was 'packaged' as *an experience*, which may once again change in the future.

Users of the AttrakDiff questionnaire (Hassenzahl et al. 2003) have been able to provide data on the interplay between variables that were generated from theory (Hassenzahl 2004b). The theory distinguishes two variables that account for the character of a product (Logan et al. 1994). This assumption is made clear in Hassenzahl's paper on the interplay of the variables, where he states that "the model assumes that two distinct attribute groups, namely 'pragmatic' and 'hedonic' attributes, can describe product characters". The variables, *hedonic-stimulation*, *hedonic-identification*, and *pragmatic-quality*, are plausible and have since found empirical data to support the claim that they could be useful constructs for exploring user experience (Hassenzahl et al. 2002). Some of these subsequent studies have used this questionnaire to build their own models of user experience (e.g. Karapanos et al. 2009; Minge 2008; Thüring and Mahlke 2007). However, what is required is an open exploration of the constructs that underlie a product's character, with no assumptions or a priori variables, and to find a way of grouping these constructs to find empirically derived super-ordinate constructs, which can then be used to measure perceived characters of products. These super constructs may then be used to make measurements at different times.

As discussed above, the appearance of an artifact is very important to the way people experience it. However, the visual aspect is also part of a complex message that has roles for the designer, artifact and consumer, including the context and environment. The product is seen as the 'transmitter' of the message, while the user is the 'receiver': "the visual appearance of products is a critical determinant of consumer response … Judgements are often made on the elegance, functionality and social significance of products based largely on visual information. These judgements relate to the perceived attributes of products" (Crilly et al. 2004). As part of their well developed framework for consumer response to the visual domain of products, Crilly et al. suggest that the visual aspects of a product communicates many types of information, such as *stereotypes*, *similar products*, *metaphors*, *character*, *conventions* and *clichés* (Crilly et al. 2004). Therefore, the early window-shopping, or catalogue browsing period in consumption, is very much part of the user experience and should not be marginalised due to the lack of physical interaction. In fact, 'interaction' does occur at this early stage, and it is born in the communicative activity and constructions that are between the designer, society and user. Of course, as implied here, constructions (e.g. stereotypes) occur before the visual messages are passed in a particular moment. In other words, investigating these constructions, in the early part of the consumption process, is just as important as exploring the physical interactions that occur once the consumer starts to use the product. Therefore, in order to measure the judgment of user experience over time, pre-interaction stages should be part of the experimental protocol, as well as the whole time range, physical time or otherwise, for the same object type. In this way, the 'whole user story' may be available for analysis in order to shed light on the various interpenetrating worlds of the user.

3.2 Methods for Measuring UX

The HCI literature has demonstrated several methods geared towards measuring user experience (see standard HCI texts, e.g. Dix et al. 2004; Sharp et al. 2007). There have also been a few attempts at categorising these methods from the standpoint of exploratory research towards theory (Väänänen-Vainio-Mattila et al. 2008), and also from the point of view of experience-centred design, where user needs are seen to be driving product design (Blyth et al. 2006). However, any method measuring UX makes assumptions about the nature of UX. In other words, each method only measures some aspects of UX. It is therefore up to the researcher to choose methods that would cover the aspects that they deem to be important. This very act of choosing is, of course, making a priori assumptions in its own right. For example, if a researcher was to only choose 'interviews' as the method of eliciting data regarding the nature of UX, then there is a fundamental assumption that participants are able to verbalise and articulate all aspects of their experience with technology. In this case, should there be a significant aspect of UX that is difficult for participants to verbalise, then the research would miss such data, because interviews rely heavily on verbal communication.

With the above caveat in mind, the following is a description of some of the main groups of methods that have already been used to explore UX. The quantitative methods tend to be associated with the 'cognitive' stance, where UX is seen as distinct collections of processes or dimensions. For example, for Lindgaard and Dudek (2002), *user satisfaction, aesthetics* and *usability* were seen as primary aspects of UX. In their study, they measured UX by varying the aesthetics of web sites, while exposing the participants to usability constraints. They then conducted interviews to discuss people's experience, and measured their satisfaction by counting positive and negative statements. In this way, they simplified, perhaps over-simplified, the experience into a number count of positive statements and then attempted to correlate the count with the variation of usability and aesthetics.

Traditional experimental psychology studies frequently employ the semantic differential (Osgood et al. 1957), where participants rate constructs or statements on a set of semantic deferential scales. This has been seen as a rudimentary, but effective method for accessing 'meaning' and how people make sense of the world. The scales are also typically used in conjunction with factor analysis to measure dimensions underlying people's ratings [e.g. Lavie and Tractinsky (2004)]. However, some of the approaches above have been accused of being too reductive (Swallow et al. 2005), and have been contrasted with the more holistic approach to the nature of UX. Jääskö and Mattelmäki (2003) proposed that UX is composed of certain aspects, as discussed in Chap. 2 (Fig. 2.1). They proceeded to test two contrasting qualitative methods to find which method was more suited to the different aspects. They suggested that UX could be explored by direct observation of participants, in an ethnographic manner. The second method was based on 'probes' (Gaver et al. 1999). In this method, the researchers provided participants (hospital workers at work) with recording devices such as a camera, audio recording etc. The researchers then made case-studies of the participants in the context of the world where they used the technology artifacts in that setting. They then made a qualitative analysis, and interpretation of the data that were collected. This 'probing' technique is particularly suited to an ethnographic type of study, where the researcher wants to understand the world that the participant is living in, without the intrusive presence of the observer. Such a technique would therefore rely on the participant ensuring data capture. This would then raise the question of consistency and reliability of the participants, as well as their 'filtering' of which data to capture, whether deliberately or not.

3.3 Measuring Dynamics of Experience

The discussions in this book have mostly focused on UX related to digital media devices, and since the dynamic aspects of UX are part of the research questions, methods that have attempted to measure these aspects are therefore of particular interest. In this context, Mahlke (2006) has undertaken a study of people's experience with physical MP3 players. His method of exploring UX was based on providing the participants with short tasks, and then asking the participants to rate the devices after interaction, later examining the correlations between the ratings of different dimensions. Though ratings were only made at a single time-point after interaction.

In contrast, using their own model of UX, Thüring and Mahlke (2007) conducted a study to establish the changes in ratings of UX dimensions as interaction takes place. However, they only measured aesthetics prior to interaction, and only measured usability after interaction, in order to find the link between perceived aesthetics and experienced usability. Increasing the timescale, Karapanos et al. (2008) also used a rating instrument, making measurements at one week after initial exposure, and then four weeks after that. However, since their rating instrument was not developed using physical devices, but was created with software products, it could therefore be missing some key aspects of experience. On an even longer timescale than the above examples, one particular study was conducted over a 'retrospective' twelve-month period (Wilamowitz-Moellendorff et al. 2006). In other words, the participants were asked to remember how they felt about a particular dimension of their experience. Such data may be criticised for its validity, as people's memories are subject to change as time goes on.

The above studies have focused their attention on a predefined idea of what UX is. However, Karapanos et al. (2009) conducted another study to examine the dynamics of UX, where data were collected using the Day Reconstruction Method (DRM), which is essentially a diary method. The study was focused on people's experience one week before they bought a mobile phone, and then four weeks after they had been using it. This is a type of an 'experience sampling' method, where the participants record a reconstruction of their day, on a daily basis. Participants also rated their experience on a concise rating instrument, as well as recorded a short narrative of their daily experience. The narratives were then subject to content analysis, as well as counting references to *satisfying* and *dissatisfying* experiences.

3.4 Measuring Users' Own Perspective

In the previous chapters, UX has been discussed in relation to the person's own, individual point of view. Specifically, it is this point of view that is of interest in this book. For this reason, case studies used here to explore UX should be anchored in a phenomenological stance. For example, discussed above, Vyas and Veer's study (2006) took a holistic approach to UX, and was based on groups of three interviews: pre-, during-, and post-interaction. Therefore, the researchers were able to account for the participants past experiences and views that would be relevant to the inter-action the participants were about to have. In this way, the data were significantly more holistic, than if only technology-centred data were collected. This way of following people's experience in a holistic way is consistent with the requirements of the research questions raised here. Importantly, the above study was conducted with PCT as a psychological theory binding its interpretation and data collection during the interviews, For example, the participants were asked about their anticipations in the first interviews, as well as subsequent ones, and their responses were then taken into account during the data analysis. This is in contrast to the study by Karapanos et al. (2009), which did not have such an underlying theory.

The main challenge regarding data obtained by open or semi-structured inter-views as described above, is the sheer mass of unstructured information. One way of dealing with such data is to systematically sift through the content in order to find recurring themes. One such method is Content Analysis, and according to Mostyn (1985), content analysis is "the diagnostic tool of qualitative researchers which they use when faced with a mass of open-ended material to make sense of. The purpose of the content analysis approach is to identify specific characteris-tics of communications systematically and objectively in order to convert the raw material into scientific data." (Mostyn 1985, p. 177). The process involves reading the corpus of the data at least once in order to get a 'feel' for the content. The next step is to find general themes by loosely classifying sections, and then to re-read the corpus to confirm the derived themes or otherwise find new or different ones. The process of classification of the data allows themes to be identified. Content analysis is by its nature hermeneutic, therefore redoing the above cycle several times is helpful towards ensuring rigorous analysis.

Grounded Theory is another method that is used to deal with large amounts of qualitative data, and as with Content Analysis, also has an element of coding for emerging themes from the data (Willig 2001). However, with Grounded Theory, early themes are taken into further data collection to explore the relationship between the themes by a process of *integration* to eventually inductively derive a theory. The theory is then intended to explain the relationship and causality between the themes. The main criticism of this method is its *positivist* stance where the researcher is seen as a 'witness' to the 'emerging' themes as something to be discovered. In contrast, Content Analysis makes no such claims on the emerging themes, and just reports over-arching categories from the data.

3.4.1 Constructs and Phenomenology

People's conceptualising and understanding of their world, and therefore their 'knowledge', may be seen as based on categorisation (see Goldstone and Kersten 2003). Such understandings are essentially the building blocks of the meanings that an user will give to a particular experience. However, a major development in psychological theory was that proposed by Kelly (1955), introducing the idea that a person is constantly updating their understanding by reconstruing their world. In support of Kelly's view, Butt (2003) has also argued that phenomenology and Personal Construct Theory (PCT) are closely linked, where PCT may "fruitfully be seen as a phenomenological approach to the person and that its methods for investigating the experience of individuals mirror and indeed extend phenomenology's reach" (Butt 2003, p. 379). Therefore, since phenomenology is the study of subjective experience, techniques that are concerned with how people categorise and understand their world are well placed for investigating people's experience with technology. Butt (2004) also makes the point that for experience, it is a matter of 'understanding it', in a holistic sense, rather than 'explaining it', in a Cartesian or cause and effect manner.

PCT can be used as a tool for the investigation of experience, by using construct elicitation methods. For example, Hassenzahl et al. (2003) used PCT-based methodology to elicit users' constructs, which were then used in a later study to access what he called the "*content* of beauty" (Hassenzahl 2004a, p. 379). In that study, he wanted to find the attributes of an artifact that people 'see' (software artifact in this particular case), which he proposed to be the attributes that people ultimately translate into subjective signs that have meaning. These attributes must have a sensorial manifestation that is objective, such as colour, shape or brand logo. Hence, it follows that these attributes can therefore be measured. However, it may be that users do not know what the attributes are, and they have to be found via methods other than asking the users. Constructs that are derived in a sorting task elucidate such objective properties, which may be visual attributes, as seen in a photograph or in a physical object, and can be merely signs to meaning. In other words, "objective qualities only serve the purpose of recognition" (Csikszentmihalyi and Rochberg-Halton 1981, p. 180).

However, other studies have also attempted to elicit the constructs that users have with respect to technological artifacts. Hassenzahl and Wessler (2000) explored the diversity of constructs for users of software products and household appliances. Their work was particularly focused on providing designers a way of exposing the users' constructs in order to advance the design process. Using such constructs also provides researchers with direct access to the 'personal constructs' that a person holds when making sense of a particular artifact, which can be turned into generalised groups of constructs that are the 'shared' constructs for that particular artifact, or group of artifacts.

The sorting of stimuli, for example, a collection of possessions, consumer products, or a group of web sites, would provide a window to the constructs that people have with such stimuli. Such a sorting task is the basis of the phenomenologically grounded technique, the Repertory Grid Test (RGT), which was developed by Kelly (1955) as part of his interest in applying his Personal Construct Theory (PCT) in a clinical setting. The technique was developed in order to help him elicit personal constructs in an interview context. Although Kelly first used this technique to understand personality differences in the construction of social perceptions, and to investigate the nature of experience, it has since been applied in a wide variety of settings, including market research and product design, including early HCI (see the special issue of the *International Journal of Man–Machine Studies* [Vol. 13(1), 1980)], and consumer products (Marsden and Littler 2000). The RGT technique has been successfully applied in a few studies to investigate such technological artifacts as web sites and search engines (Hassenzahl and Trautmann 2001; Johnson and Crudge 2007; Tan and Tung 2003), and some concerned with the design and evaluation of digital interactive devices (Fallman 2006a; Hassenzahl and Wessler 2000). Or compare virtual and real objects in a domain (Sener et al. 2006).

The RGT technique involves eliciting constructs by asking participants to sort 'triads' of stimuli, in order to verbalise their similarities and differences. For example, item A and B are similar because they are 'round', while they are different to item C, because it is 'angular'. Therefore, the construct of 'roundness' is a polar opposite of 'angular'. The participant is then asked to indicate the desirable pole of the construct, i.e. whichever of the poles is the one that has positive connotations. This elicitation is done many times with several objects to obtain as many constructs as the participant is able to verbalise. In this way, the researcher is able to derive structured qualitative data. The participant is then asked to rate each of the items on a differential scale between the poles of the construct. The result is a grid of all the constructs, and all the elements (the items), with a rating for each element. This grid is then considered to be a representation of the participants' view of the domain of elements presented to them. The grid could then be used in an interview that is structured around the grid, e.g. to discuss why the ratings are the way they are. Also, the grid can be used to represent the data in a two dimensional view (Fallman and Waterworth 2005).

However, in their conclusions, Sener et al. (2006) confirm one of the significant drawbacks of using this method effectively, is that the "[RGT] technique and the subsequent analysis procedure described, required substantial exertion of time and effort by the research team" (Sener et al. 2006, p. 153). This issue could provide real restrictions on using this method with certain groups, e.g. children, or participants with low attention span. Also, the tedious nature of the RGT method and length of time it takes to administer (and analyse) could also have adverse effects on the quality of the data. Also, another common problem for the RGT is that of verbalisation. Participants cannot always say what they mean. However, even if they were able to, another criticism is regarding the meaning of constructs or verbalisations; people may mean different things when saying the same thing [see for example, Boehner (2006) criticising Fallman's RGT based study (Boehner 2006)]. In fact, such criticism is aimed at the internal validity of *any* qualitative study, and not specific to RGT. In other words, a researcher can never know what a participant really means, even when they try to explain it.

3.4.2 Sorting Categories

The above critiques of the repertory grid test have led to new variations, and one such critique is made by Canter et al. (1985). Along with the disadvantages shown above, they point out that the RGT method, as well as the semantic differential, both make the assumption that user constructs are polar (e.g. usable versus awkward), and therefore asks participants to make polar judgements regarding categorisation. However, people's categorisations do not necessarily fall along such singular dimensions.

They also point out that the original RGT was designed at a time when the available statistical tests for analysing it were limited. They recommend a variation on the RGT, which is a more open ended sorting of multiple items with no restrictions on the type of constructs generated or the distribution of the category assignments. Their own technique is a Multiple Sorting Procedure (MSP) designed as the focus of a broader interview about personal interpretations of items. It involves presenting people with a large set of items which can be grouped into as many different piles as they like, as many times as they can. After each sort, participants are interviewed about the reasons for their classifications and the way in which groups are similar or different from each other. Multidimensional Scalogram Analysis (MSA) is then performed on the resulting sort data, to yield spatial maps of constructs for interpretation alongside interview discussions. As Hassenzahl and Wessler suggested, "a method should be able to capture relations between single constructs, for example as a hierarchical or network structure." (Hassenzahl and Wessler 2000, p. 458). The spatial maps from the MSP

combination with MSA do exactly that. They show the sorted items, or technological artifacts, to be localised according to the similarity in the way participants
viewed them. For this reason, the MSA is advantageous over techniques such as
Principle Component Analysis (PCA) because it highlights the complex relationship between constructs over a two dimensional space, rather than simply relay
correlation ures between components in the dataset (for further discussions on
card-sorting see Spencer 2009; Tullis and Albert 2008, p. 222).

A technique which combines MSP with MSA or Smallest Space Analysis
(SSA), has been used to good effect in examining people's understanding of
a wide range of different stimuli (Barnett 2004; Wilson 1995). This method can
therefore be applied to explore people's conceptualisation of media players, as
exemplars of mobile technology. Life-size photographs of different MP3 players
could be used as stimuli to be sorted into piles. A sorting criterion is then equivalent to a construct, and the label for each pile is equivalent to a category. A construct could be for example "usability", whereas a category would be "awkward"
or "easy to use". This approach allows researchers access to how users conceptualise specific artifacts, thereby giving the researchers the opportunity to 'see' what
the users 'see' and what they pay attention to, explicitly or otherwise, across similar artifacts. The method also involves talking to participants about the reasons for
their sorts, giving further insight into their subjective construction of similarity and
difference between the items. Therefore, employing such an approach can enhance
the researchers' ability to understand the users' lifeworld.

Personal constructs exist in any realm where an user understands something,
or makes sense of it. This means that this method can be applied to objects, pictures of objects, screenshots of web pages, abstract ideas and even experiences
themselves (summarised on a card). In fact, the use of photographs in simulat-
ing environments has been shown to be a valid replacement for real environments
(Stamps 1990). Therefore, it would be fair to assume the same would be true for
photographs of other 'environments', such as technology. Therefore, if an user can
sort the entity into piles, that means they are organising these entities into categories of a particular construct.

The use of MSP in combination with MDS variants (e.g. SSA), is part of the
Facet Theory 'theory building' approach. A main defining feature of Facet Theory,
originally developed by Guttman (1954), is that it is a meta-theory, i.e. it is a
theory about theory, and as such is used to derive theory from data, rather than
impose one a priori. This is a particularly important point because it addresses
the main issues raised so far, where most other theories of UX have been created
on the basis of previous assumptions of what UX should or should not be (e.g.
Hassenzahl 2004b; Karapanos et al. 2009).

In summary then, aesthetics has been shown to be a recurring construct in UX.
Nonetheless, the relationships between aesthetics and other aspects of UX have
so far been inconclusive. Tractinsky et al. (2000) showed a positive correlation
between beauty and usability, and Thüring and Mahlke (2007) confirmed that non-
instrumental qualities have a role to play in overall judgement. However, although,
Hassenzahl's (2004b) results showed no association between actual experience of

usability and beauty, they did show that hedonic attributes and beauty aspects were stable over time, while Minge (2008) showed that, for virtual technology, attractiveness tended to overshadow perceived usability before use, but has less of an overshadowing effect after use. Therefore, given the complexity of relationships between UX attributes reported in the literature, and the apparent contradictions, these complex relationships may benefit from further study. In particular, the modulating effect of time and interaction on these relationships might be illuminated by considering UX attributes as evolving personal constructs.

With regards to the dynamics of UX, Karapanos et al. (2009) used physical devices and were able to confirm Berlyne's (1970) earlier data regarding the reduction of stimulation through time (e.g. novelty), they were unable to distinguish between types of constructs that were more or less susceptible to change through interaction. However, although Minge (2008) explored the changes in UX between pre- and post-interaction, this was only done for 'virtual' devices, which leaves the 'physical' aspect of interaction unaccounted for. Therefore, none of the above studies explored the changes in UX as users move from a purely visual pre-interactive experience, to first-time physical interaction, which is the kind of experience that is pervasive and common for mobile media technologies, and technology in general. Therefore, in trying to answer some of the questions raised in this chapter, and as *meaning* is so central to the concept of *experience*, it is important to explore experimental methods that are well suited to measuring *meaning*. Equally important is the sense of change in meaning, the dynamics of user experience. This chapter therefore confirms the importance of the first and second research questions highlighted earlier regarding meaning-making, and underlying constructs in UX. However, this chapter also raises a third research question about how construction of meaning changes over time.

As discussed above, UX has both qualitative and quantitative aspects, and any attempt to measure UX must be sympathetic to both. Therefore, it seems that a reasoned way forward to address the research questions is to take advantage of the different approaches and methods described above, and use a combined approach that would explore UX from different perspectives. This combination of methodologies would be more likely to pickup different aspects of UX, without the polarised limitations of one technique or method. Therefore, in order to maintain an open and exploratory outlook to this investigation, both quantitative and qualitative methods will be explored, while maintaining a strong phenomenological basis. The next chapters will show implementation of these methods, producing combined data-sets to be discussed in the context of the ICE model of User Experience.

References

Asch, S. E. (1946). Forming impressions of personality. *Journal of Abnormal and Social Psychology, 41*, 258–290.

Barnett, J. (2004). The multiple sorting procedure (MSP). In G. M. Breakwell (Ed.), *Doing social psychology research* (pp. 289–304). Oxford: BPS Blackwell.

Battarbee, K., & Mattelmäki, T. (2002). *Meaningful relationships with products*. Paper presented at the Proceedings of the Design and Emotions Conference, Loughborough.

Belk, R. W. (1988). Possessions and the extended self. *Journal of Consumer Research, 15*(2), 139–168.

Berlyne, D. E. (1960). *Conflict, arousal and curiosity*. New York: McGraw-Hill.

Berlyne, D. E. (1970). Novelty, complexity and hedonic value. *Perception and Psychophysics, 8*, 279–286.

Berlyne, D. E. (1974). *Studies in the new experimental aesthetics: Steps toward an objective psychology of aesthetic appreciation*. Washington: Halsted Press.

Blyth, M. A., Wright, P. C., McCarthy, J., & Bertelsen, O. W. (2006). *Theory and method for experience centred design*, Montréal.

Boehner, K. (2006). *Experiencing evaluation: Paths, borders and guides*. Paper presented at the Theory and Method for Experience Centred Design Workshop—CHI2006.

Butt, T. (2003). The phenomenological context of personal construct psychology. In F. Fransella (Ed.), *International handbook of personal construct psychology* (pp. 379–386). Chichester: Wiley.

Butt, T. (2004). Understanding, explanation and personal constructs. *Personal Construct Theory and Practice, 1*, 21–27.

Canter, D., Brown, J., & Groat, L. (1985). A multiple sorting procedure. In M. Brenner, J. Brown, & D. Canter (Eds.), *The research interview: Uses and approaches*. London: Academic Press.

Castro, J. F., Perez, R. G., Barrantes, N., & Capdevila, A. (1998). Mood state and recall biases: The role of affect. *Psychology in Spain, 2*(1), 92–99.

Chua, S. L., Chen, D.-T., & Wong, A. F. L. (1999). Computer anxiety and its correlates: A meta-analysis. *Computers in Human Behavior, 15*(5), 609–623.

Crilly, N., Moultrie, J., & Clarkson, P. J. (2004). Seeing things: Consumer response to the visual domain in product design. *Design Studies, 25*(6), 547–577.

Csikszentmihalyi, M. (1990). *Flow: The psychology of optimal experience*. New York: Harper Collins.

Csikszentmihalyi, M., & Rochberg-Halton, E. (1981). *The meaning of things*. Cambridge: Cambridge University Press.

Dion, K., Berscheid, E., & Walster, E. (1972). What is beautiful is good. *Journal of Personality and Social Psychology, 24*(3), 285–290.

Dittmar, H. (1992). *The social psychology of material possessions: To have is to be*. New York: St. Martin's Press.

Dix, A., Finlay, J., Abowd, G. D., & Beale, R. (2004). *Human-computer interaction* (3rd ed.). Harlow: Pearson Education.

Fallman, D. (2006a). *Catching the interactive experience: Using the repertory grid technique for qualitative and quantitative insight into user experience*. Paper presented at the Proceedings of Engage: Interaction, Art, and Audience Experience, Sydney.

Fallman, D., & Waterworth, J. (2005). *Dealing with user experience and affective evaluation in HCI design: A repertory grid approach*. Paper presented at the Workshop on Evaluation of Affective Interfaces, Conference on Human Factors in Computing Systems, CHI 2005, Portland, Oregon.

Forlizzi, J., & Ford, S. (2000). *The building blocks of experience: An early framework for interaction designers*. Paper presented at The Conference on Designing Interactive Systems: Processes, Practices, Methods, And Techniques, New York.

Frohlich, D. (2004). Beauty as a design prize. *Human-Computer Interaction, 19*, 359–366.

Gaver, W., Dunne, T., & Pacenti, E. (1999). Design: Cultural probes. *Interactions, 6*(1), 21–29.

Goldstone, R. L., & Kersten, A. (2003). Concepts and categorization. In A. F. Healy & R. W. Proctor (Eds.), *Comprehensive handbook of psychology* (Vol. 4, pp. 599–621)., Experimental psychology(22) New Jersey: Wiley.

Groves, P. M., & Thompson, R. F. (1970). Habituation: a dual process theory. *Psychological Review, 77*(5), 419–450.

Guttman, L. (1954). A new approach to factor analysis: The radex. In P. F. Lazarfeld (Ed.), *Mathematical thinking in the social sciences*. New York: Free Press.

Hartman, J., Sutcliffe, A., & de Angeli, A. (2008). Towards a theory of user judgment of aesthetics and user interface quality. *Transactions on Computer-Human Interaction (TOCHI), 15*(4), 15.

Hassenzahl, M. (2001). The effect of perceived hedonic quality on product appealingness. *International Journal of Human-Computer Interaction, 13*(4), 481–499.

Hassenzahl, M. (2004). The interplay of beauty, goodness, and usability in interactive products. *Human-Computer Interactions, 19*, 319–349.

Hassenzahl, M., & Trautmann, T. (2001). *Analysis of web sites with the repertory grid technique.* Paper presented at the Conference on Human Factors in Computing Systems—CHI'01 Extended Abstract.

Hassenzahl, M., & Wessler, R. (2000). Capturing design space from a user perspective: the repertory grid technique revisited. *International Journal of Human-Computer Interaction, 12*(3/4), 441–459.

Hassenzahl, M., Kekez, R., & Burmester, M. (2002). *The importance of a software's pragmatic quality depends on usage modes.* Paper presented at the 6th International Conference on Work with Display Units (WWDU 2002), Berlin.

Hassenzahl, M., Burmester, M., & Koller, F. (2003). AttrakDiff: Ein Fragebogen zur Messung wahrgenommener hedonischer und pragmatischer Qualität (AttracDiff: A questionnaire to measure perceived hedonic and pragmatic quality). In J. Ziegler & G. Szwillus (Eds.), *Mensch & Computer 2003. Interaktion in Bewegung* (pp. 187–196). Stutgart, Leipzig: Teubner.

Isen, A. M. (1990). The influence of positive and negative affect on cognitive organization: Some implications for development. In N. Stein, L. B. Leventhal, & T. Trabasso (Eds.), *Psychological and biological approaches to emotion* (pp. 75–94). Hillsdale: Lawrence Erlbaum.

ISO-9241-11. (1998). Guidance on usability.

Jääskö, V., & Mattelmäki, T. (2003). *Observing and probing.* Paper presented at the Proceedings of the 2003 International Conference on Designing Pleasurable Products and Interfaces, Pittsburgh.

Johnson, F. C., & Crudge, S. E. (2007). Using the repertory grid and laddering techniques to determine the user's evaluative model of search engines. *Journal of Documentation, 63*(2), 259–280.

Kaplan, R., & Kaplan, S. (1989). *The experience of nature: A psychological perspective.* New York: Cambridge University Press.

Karapanos, E., Hassenzahl, M., & Martens, J.-B. (2008). *User experience over time.* Paper presented at the CHI 2008—Work in Progress, Florence, Italy.

Karapanos, E., Zimmerman, J., Forlizzi, J., & Martens, J.-B. (2009). *User experience over time: An initial framework.* Paper presented at The CHI Conference on Computer-Human Interaction—SIG, Boston, USA.

Kelly, G. A. (1955). *The psychology of personal constructs, vol. 1: Theory and personality* (1991 ed. vol. 1). London: Routledge.

Kumar, V. (2013). *101 design methods: A structured approach for driving innovation in your organisation.* Hoboken: Wiley.

Kurosu, M., & Kashimura, K. (1995). *Apparent usability vs. inherent usability: experimental analysis on the determinants of the apparent usability.* Paper presented at the Proceedings of the SIGCHI conference on Human factors in computing systems, Denver, Colorado, United States.

Lang, J. (1988). Symbolic aesthetics in architecture: Toward a research agenda. In J. L. Nasar (Ed.), *Environmental aesthetics: Theory, research and applications* (pp. 11–26). Cambridge: Cambridge University Press.

Lavie, T., & Tractinsky, N. (2004). Assessing dimensions of perceived visual aesthetics of web sites. *International Journal of Human-Computer Studies, 60*, 269–298.

Lindgaard, G., & Dudek, C. (2002). *User satisfaction, aesthetics and usability: Beyond reductionism.* Paper presented at the Proceedings IFIP 17th World Computer Congress, Montreal, Canada.

Lindgaard, G., Fernandes, G., Dudek, C., & Brown, J. (2006). Attention web designers: You have 50 milliseconds to make a good first impression! *Behaviour and Information Technology, 25*(2), 115–126.

Logan, R. J., Augaitis, S. R., & Renk, T. (1994). *Design of simplified television remote controls: A case for behavioral and emotional usability.* Paper presented at the Human Factors and Ergonomics Society 38th Annual Meeting, Santa Monica, CA.

Lynch, K. (1960). *The image of the city.* Cambridge: MIT Press.

Mahlke, S. (2006). *Aesthetic and symbolic qualities as antecedents of overall judgements of interactive products.* Paper presented at the People and Computers XX—Engage: HCI 2006, London.

Mandler, G. (1990). A constructivist theory of emotion. In N. L. Stein, B. Leventhal, & T. Trabasso (Eds.), *Psychological and biological approaches to emotion* (pp. 21–43). Hillsdale: Lawrence Erlbaum.

Marsden, D., & Littler, D. (2000). Exploring consumer product construct systems with the repertory grid technique. *Qualitative Market Research: An International Journal, 3*(3), 127–144.

McCarthy, J., & Wright, P. C. (2004). *Technology as experience.* Cambridge: MIT Press.

McClelland, D. C., Atkinson, J. W., Clark, R. A., & Lowell, E. L. (1953). *The achievement motive.* New York: Appleton-Century-Crofts.

Mehrabian, A., & Russell, J. A. (1974). *An approach to environmental psychology.* Cambridge: MIT Press.

Mendoza, V., & Novick, D. G. (2005). *Usability over time.* Paper presented at the 23rd Annual International Conference on Design of Communication: Documenting and Designing for Pervasive Information, Coventry, UK.

Minge, M. (2008). *Dynamics of user experience.* Paper presented at the Research Goals and Strategies for Studying User Experience and Emotion—NordiCHI2008, Lund, Sweden.

Mostyn, B. (1985). The content analysis of qualitative research data: A dynamic approach. In M. Brenner, J. Brown, & D. Canter (Eds.), *The research interview: Uses and approaches* (pp. 115–145). London: Academic Press.

Norman, D. A. (2004). Introduction to this special section on beauty, goodness, and usability. *Human-Computer Interaction, 19*, 311–318.

Osgood, C. E., Suci, G. J., & Tannenbaum, P. H. (1957). *The measurement of meaning.* Urbana: Illinois University Press.

Prentice, D. A. (1987). Psychological correspondence of possessions, attitudes, and values. *Journal of Personality and Social Psychology, 53*(6), 993–1003.

Purcell, A. T. (1986). Environmental perception and affect: A schema discrepancy model. *Environment and Behavior, 18*(1), 3–30.

Purcell, A. T., & Nasar, J. L. (1992). Experiencing other peoples houses: A model of similarities and differences in environmental experience. *Journal of Environmental Psychology, 12*, 199–211.

Rafaeli, A., & Vilnai-Yavetz, I. (2004). Instrumentality, aesthetics and symbolism of physical artifacts astriggers of emotion. *Theoretical Issues in Ergonomics Science, 5*(1), 91–112.

Rholes, W. S., Riskind, J. H., & Lane, J. W. (1987). Emotional states and memory biases: Effects of cognitive priming and mood. *Journal of Personality and Social Psychology, 52*(1), 91–99.

Richins, M. L. (1994). Valuing things: The public and private meanings of possessions. *Journal of Consumer Research, 21*(3), 504–521.

Russell, P. A. (2000). Testing the aesthetic significance of the golden-section rectangle. *Perception, 29*(12), 1413–1422.

Sener, B., Gültekin, P., & Erbug, Ç. (2006). Comparisons between user expectations for products in physical and virtual domains. In P. D. Bust (Ed.), *Contemporary ergonomics 2006* (pp. 149–156). Great Britain: Taylor & Francis.

Sharp, H., Rogers, Y., & Preece, J. (2007). *Interaction design: Beyond human-computer interaction.* Chichester: Wiley.

Silverstone, R., & Haddon, L. (1996). Design and the domestication of information and communication technologies: Technical change and everyday life. In R. Mansell & R. Silverstone (Eds.), *Communication by design: The politics of information and communication technologies* (pp. 44–74). USA: Oxford University Press.

de Souza, C. S. (2005). *The semiotic engineering of human-computer interaction.* Cambridge: The MIT Press.

Spencer, D. (2009). *Card sorting: Designing usable categories Brooklyn.* New York: Rosenfeld Media.

Stamps, A. E. (1990). Use of photographs to simulate environments: a meta-analysis. *Perceptual and Motor Skills, 71,* 907–913.

Swallow, D., Blyth, M. A., & Wright, P. C. (2005). *Grounding experience: Relating theory and method to evaluate the user experience of smartphones.* Paper presented at the Proceedings of the 2005 Annual Conference on European Association of Cognitive Ergonomics.

Tan, F. B., & Tung, L. L. (2003). *Exploring website evaluation criteria using the repertory grid technique: A web designers' perspective.* Paper presented at the SIGHCI 2003.

Thorndike, E. L. (1920). A constant error on psychological rating. *Journal of Applied Psychology, 4*(1), 25–29.

Thüring, M., & Mahlke, S. (2007). Usability, aesthetics, and emotions in human-technology-interaction. *International Journal of Psychology, 42,* 253–264.

Tractinsky, N., Shoval-Katz, A., & Ikar, D. (2000). What is beautiful is usable. *Interacting with Computers, 13,* 127–145.

Tullis, T., & Albert, B. (2008). *Measuring the user experience: Collecting, analyzing, and presenting usability metrics.* Burlington: Morgan Kaufman.

Väänänen-Vainio-Mattila, K., Roto, V., & Hassenzahl, M. (2008). *Now let's do it in practice: User experience evaluation methods in product development.* Paper presented at the Conference on Human Factors in Computing Systems, Florence, Italy.

Vyas, D., & van der Veer, G. C. (2006). *Rich evaluations of entertainment experience—bridging the interpretational gap.* Paper presented at the 13th European Conference on Cognitive Ergonomics: Trust and Control in Complex Socio-Technical Systems, Zurich, Switzerland.

Walker, E. L. (1973). Psychological complexity and preference. In D. E. Berlyne & K. B. Madsen (Eds.), *Pleasure, reward, preference: Their nature, determinants and role in behavior.* New York: Academic Press.

Wallendorf, M., Belk, R. W., & Heisley, D. (1988). Deep meaning in possessions: The Paper. *Advances in Consumer Research, 15,* 528–530.

Wilamowitz-Moellendorff, von M., Hassenzahl, M., & Platz, A. (2006). *Dynamics of user experience: How the perceived quality of mobile phones changes over time.* Paper presented at the User Experience: Towards a Unified View—COST294-MAUSE.

Willig, C. (2001). *Introducing qualitative research in psychology: Adventures in theory and method.* Maidenhead: Open University Press.

Wilson, M. (1995). Structuring qualitative data: Multidimensional scalogram analysis. In G. Breakwell, S. Hammond, & C. Fife-Shaw (Eds.), *Research methods in psychology.* London: Sage Publications.

Yerkes, R. M., & Dodson, J. D. (1908). The relation of strength of stimulus to rapidity of habit-formation. *Journal of Comparative Neurology and Psychology, 18*(459), 482.

Zajonc, R. B. (1980). Feeling and thinking: Preferences need no inferences. *American Psychologist, 35*(2), 151–175.

Chapter 4
Construct Dynamics: Interaction

Abstract In order to gain further understanding of the basic building blocks of user experience, this chapter focuses on short-term dynamics as explored in two case-studies. The first is designed to elicit personal constructs related to how people experience mobile media devices using a technique which combines the Multiple Sorting Procedure (MSP) with Multidimensional Scalogram Analysis (MSA), both closely connected to Personal Construct Theory. The study yields preference dimensions using both qualitative and quantitative insights into how users make sense of their experiences, as well as the classification of constructs into five super-constructs, or five dimensions of UX: *Novelty*, *Usability*, *Complexity*, *Aesthetics* and *Physicality*. These data are then used as the foundations for a subsequent case-study aimed at identifying super-constructs that describe primary dimensions of user experience. The data in the second case-study demonstrate clear two-dimensional relationships between the constructs (especially in terms of aesthetics) as users move from pre- to post-interaction, as well as contributing to the development of a high reliability UX-Scale.

Keywords Human–Computer interaction (HCI) • Mobile device usability • Multiple sorting procedure (MSP) • Multidimensional scalogram analysis (MSA) • Smallest space analysis (SSA) • Personal Construct Theory (PCT) • User experience (UX) • User experience dynamics • UX-scale

Chapters 2 and 3 have provided a review of theories and previous studies investigating User Experience, including the 'qualities' of UX, UX as a 'consequence' of interacting with technology, and the 'processes' that people use to make sense of 'threads' of UX. Chapter 2 concluded with *ICE* as a proposed model of UX, that sees *interaction*, *construction* and *evaluation* as the primary processes. Construction is seen here in the way that is described by Kelly (1955), and is considered to be a central theme in UX, and the sense-making process that underpins UX.

Those reviews led to three research questions. The first question is related to how users create meaning through their experience with technology, while the second question is about the nature of UX and its underlying constructs. The third question is regarding the change in meaning and constructs over time, specifically during consumption of technology. Consumption was shown to be a cycle of phases that can be described as: *Approach*, *Buying*, *Consummation* and *Dissolution*. This book will therefore draw on the methods outlined in Chap. 3, to explore these questions as UX evolves along the consumption phases. This chapter is concerned with exploring the research questions for the earliest period of intended interaction, *Approach*. Therefore, the first task is to consider the nature of the constructs people apply in their understanding of the technology.

The example of technology that is used here is *mobile media players*, specifically, MP3 music players. These devices were selected as the target technology because they embody a range of aesthetic and functional properties that have already been researched and discussed in the context of UX (e.g. Hassenzahl 2004). They are also widely used and so are a form of technology that most people will already have an understanding of in relation to their lives. Such technology is also popular with students who form a relatively homogeneous group of users. MP3 players are also somewhat fluid in terms of functionality and form with respect to broader classes of media players and mobile phones, which allows for a richer set of data. This was especially the case at the outset of this research project in 2005, although this aspect is evolving fast. This study was also designed to contribute to an on-going debate about the nature of beauty with regards to technological artifacts (Frohlich 2004; Hassenzahl 2004; Norman 2004). For this reason, this study also explores how participants conceptualise 'beauty' for technological devices such as MP3 players. This exploration can then be compared to how people conceptualise MP3 players in general.

In his study of software MP3 players, Hassenzahl (2004) used a rating scale, AttrakDiff (Hassenzahl et al. 2003), that was initially developed in relation to constructs that were based on interactive products in general. The scale was initially derived by group consensus from six software designers, suggesting "adjective pairs" to describe aspects of interactive products, in a focus-group setting. The scale was then modified on the basis of 22 lay-participants' judgements in a web site evaluation study. Principle Component Analysis (PCA) was then used to derive the scale dimensions. However, since the original adjectives were generated by experts, they may not be those that ordinary people would choose to apply to physical MP3 players. Further, they were not elicited in relation to the technology used in this research. Therefore, in order to elicit a set of constructs that are applicable to the technology being used in this research, the first methodological challenge is to explore how people themselves conceptualise these devices. This will allow the current research to be informed by the participants' own structure of their experiences.

4.1 User Constructs (Case-Study 1)

Therefore, the first step to take is to examine a study to explore users' constructs. This is done by focussing on the early user experience (i.e. approach and pre-interaction), involving the visual stimuli related to experience. This accesses users' initial impressions of MP3 players from the perception of their visual appearance alone, as in window or catalogue shopping, including online experiences. The visual stimuli used here are a range of photographs of devices presented on cards and the methodology chosen is a free and structured card-sorting task.

This study is described in detail elsewhere (Al-Azzawi et al. 2007). However, it is useful to give a summary of the method and primary findings here. Thirty six university students volunteered to take part in entire study, chosen to have relatively homogeneous and comparable SES and cultural backgrounds (lived in the United Kingdom since childhood). For the first part of the study, each participant was given 35 cards that showed a good quality, colour, life-sized photograph of one hand-held mobile MP3 player (Appendix-A). The MP3 players were chosen from the offering that was current and available in the market, and were chosen to be as broad a range as possible. Data were collected using the Multiple-Sorting Procedure (MSP) (Canter et al 1985), with explorative interviews at the end of each sorting section. Here, the MSP was run in three modes: free-sort, semi-structured sort and structured sort. In the free-sort mode, the participants were asked to sort the cards by *any* criteria (constructs), into *any* number of piles and placing *any* number of cards into each pile. The participants then attributed labels (categories) to each pile and explained their rationale. In the semi-structured mode, the participants were given the sorting criteria (in this case 'Kinds of Beauty'), and then they were asked to sort the cards into *any* number of piles with *any* number of cards in each pile. In the structured sort, the participants were given the sorting criteria, in this case "preference", and the number of piles and the meaning for each pile (in this case it was a 7-point preference scale), without restrictions on the number of cards per pile.

The free-sorting task was used to elicit the general constructs for mobile media devices. Once items were sorted, the participant was then asked to clarify the basis of the sort, and to give a description for each of the groups within it. For each group, item codes are noted. For more 'subjective' sorts, such as "easy to use", the participants were asked to elaborate on the choices made. Open questions were used such as "what is it about these items that make them easy to use?" Participants performed free sorts more than once, for as many times as they felt able to find new sorting criteria. Table 4.1 presents a complete list of the constructs that emerged, ordered according to how many times they were referenced as the reason for grouping. If a participant referenced more than one construct as a reason for creating a group, then each construct was credited with a reference. As an example, a participant might have said "this pile has large players with round controls", then the count for references to "controls" was incremented by one, as well as the count for references to "size" (MP3 player size). Table 4.1 shows a mixture of objective and subjective constructs.

Table 4.1 Constructs used by participants in all the 'free sorts' (Al-Azzawi et al. 2007)

No.	Construct	References	No.	Construct	References
1	Screen	44	14	Watch	8
2	Size	29	15	Headphones	8
3	Controls	26	16	Cross-linking	6
4	Shape	25	17	iPod	6
5	Colour	24	18	Orientation	6
6	Aesthetics	22	19	Construction quality	5
7	Brand	18	20	Sport	5
8	Design	17	21	Age	4
9	Functions	17	22	Gender	4
10	Usability	17	23	Weight	3
11	Convenience	14	24	Texture	1
12	Buy	11	25	Battery	1
13	Price	11	–	–	–

The 'cross-linking' construct refers to situations where a participant described the sorting criterion (the construct) in one way, and the individual categories within the construct in another. For example, participant P-02 used the construct "Sport" and the categories within the sort were "light and heavy".

An interesting finding is the strong link between perceived specifications in relation to the participants interpretation of the photographs. Even though the instructions for sorting were clear regarding the functional specifications (to ignore them), many participants still inferred or hypothesised specifications in the sorting task. Participant P-06 said that it would "not make sense" to sort them without including what he could assume, or remember about, the functional specifications of the items he was seeing. What was also interesting about this particular session with P-06 is that he insisted that he was making logical judgements about the specifications throughout most of the session, and he chose item number 17 as his favourite, with reasons such as "well designed", "good size" and "solid state" [referring to the technology type]. However, when asked: "would you still like it if it was green?" the answer was an instant "No!"

In order to detect the underlying objective structure for the sorting choices, the free-sort data were analysed by Multidimensional Scalogram Analysis (MSA) (Wilson 1995; Zvulun 1978). MSA provides a plot of all the MP3 players as points in geometric space, such that the more frequently two items are placed in the same category during the sorting task, the closer together they are in the plot. It would be reasonable to assume that these relative positions relate to an underlying physically visible property that influenced the participants, knowingly or otherwise, irrespective of the overt reason that a participant might give for placing an item in a category. Figure 4.2 shows the MSA plot from data obtained in the first sort (of the free-sorts) by all participants. These data reflect the first impressions experienced by the participants. It is divided into four regions given labels that are an interpretation by the researcher, derived from the aggregate of the

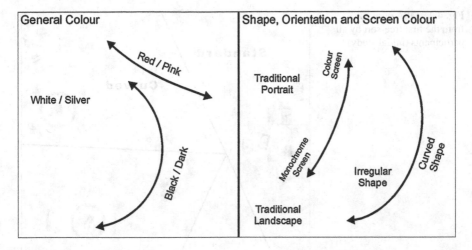

Fig. 4.1   SSA schematic, showing general preference trends (Al-Azzawi et al. 2007)

constructs that the participants gave for the individual items. These four regions can be grouped into two: simple (standard and horizontal) and non-simple (curved and other) designs

A similar sorting task was conducted to elicit participants' conceptualisations about what makes an MP3 player 'beautiful'. This time the MSP was run in a semi-structured sorting mode. The 'Kinds of Beauty' sort showed a very large range of ways of describing beauty categories and attributes (59 different constructs). This data also showed common beauty categories along with idiosyncratic ones that only appear once amongst all the participants. MSA was also carried out on the 'Kinds of Beauty' data, showing four main regions. The interpretation of the plot is consistent with general discussions with the participants in which there were regular references to "curved" and "shapely" shapes, and also "very standard", "average", "stereotypical" and "MP3 player look". The items in the 'functional' group were also given names such as "tough", "dull", "male" and "old". As with Fig. 4.2, the 'beauty' MSA can also be reduced to two main groups: simple (functional and standard), and non-simple (odd and curved). This would suggest a similarity between 'beauty' and the first-impression that users have when free-sorting photographs of MP3 players.

The participants were finally asked to sort the cards according to preference, on a scale of 1–7. The data were analysed using Smallest Space Analysis (SSA). SSA is a nonmetric MDS (Multidimensional Scaling) technique that represents variables as points in geometric space. The distance between the points is inversely proportional to the rank order of the associations between the variable. This means that the closer the points the more associated are the variables they represent. Figure 4.1 shows the trends observable in the SSA plot. There is a red/pink colour gradient across the plot, and there is also a screen colour variation (blue/dark screen at the bottom, and lighter/colourful screen at the top). There is also an orientation

Fig. 4.2 MSA derived
from the first free-sort by all
participants (initial study)

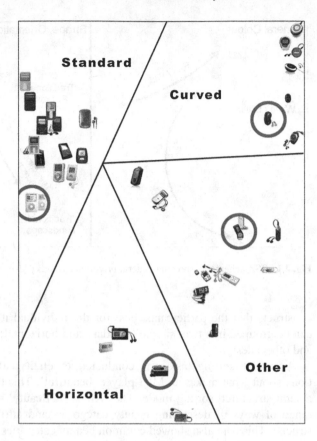

variation (landscape vs. portrait) and also a curved/small band that skirts the out-side of the plot on the right.

Further composite analysis shows that among the present group of participants (Al-Azzawi et al. 2007), there appear to be two general groups of MP3 players that are preferred. The first group are primarily rectangular and do not tend to use colours beyond black, white and silver. In contrast, the other group are pri-marily curved and with unusual shapes that use fun imagery and some colour. Interestingly, this corresponds to the distinction between Modernism and Post-Modernism found to underlie architectural preference in Wilson's (1996) study.

4.2 Construct Dynamics During Interaction (Case-Study 2)

The previous study was successful in eliciting directly relevant constructs that participants used to conceptualise MP3 players during the Approach phase of consumption. The study also confirmed findings of other research, and found aesthetics-related constructs (e.g. Tractinsky et al. 2000). However, it is possible that these constructs form larger groups or classes of constructs that are akin to Kelly's *core constructs* (1955, p. 356). Some research has suggested that UX-related constructs are divided into groups such as *hedonic* and *pragmatic*, which are based on theoretical assumptions made by Logan et al. (1994), or 'instrumental' and 'non-instrumental' groups (Hassenzahl and Tractinsky 2006), Such classifications may or may not necessarily be the users' view and further work is required in order to gain a broader understanding of the classes of constructs from the users' perspective. Also, the qualitative relationship between such classes of constructs is also unknown.

Since interaction is a major component of UX (see ICE model in Chap. 2), it is important to investigate the effects of interaction on UX, and specifically on the abovementioned constructs. Some work has already been undertaken to investigate people's rating of constructs after interaction. For example, Mahlke (2006) asked participants to rate MP3 players using a pre-existing rating scale [AttrakDiff (Hassenzahl et al. 2003)]. Participants were only asked to rate the devices *after* physical interaction during pre-set tasks. However, Minge (2008) measured participants ratings before and after interaction, but used virtual devices on a touch-screen, as did Thüring and Mahlke (2007). This still leaves the question regarding the transition between a purely visual stimulus, to a physical interaction; specifically for a first-time interaction. This is of course a special case that is nonetheless a common occurrence in people's experience with technology. Such a scenario occurs, for example, after viewing a photograph of a device on paper advertisement, and then physically interacting with the device that is in a shop or belonging to a friend. The question still remains regarding the stability of ratings. In other words, are users' ratings more likely to change for some constructs, after the transition to physical interaction, than they might for another group of constructs?

Hence, in this study, the focus of attention is on the Buying phase, which is where the transition between the Approach and Consummation phases occurs, i.e. pre- and post-interaction. This study uses rating-scales as well as post-session interviews to address all the research questions to explore how meaning making takes place in the context of the nature of the constructs of UX. The study is conducted during the special case in the dynamics of UX, where intended consumption is *actualised*.

4.2.1 Method

In the current study, participants viewed a life-sized photograph of an MP3 player, and then rated the photograph on a set of 87 UX-related constructs. They were then given the actual device, and allowed to use it, and then asked to rate the actual device for the same constructs. This was done for four devices.

The constructs that were elicited in the first study were used for the adjective rating scales for this study. Between the free-sorts and the beauty sorts, a total of

66 constructs were successfully elicited. For example *shape, size, colour, usability, weight, compactness, complexity, novelty, aesthetics, practicality, futuristic* and *brand*. These constructs were converted for use in this study. For example, "convenience", was converted to a seven point Likert rating scale phrases as "Convenient to use". Users were asked to rate the sample products on each adjective indicating the extent to which they *strongly agreed* (7) to *strongly disagreed* (1) that with the construct applied to each device.

Other constructs were converted to their component elements, e.g. "gender" was converted to "masculine" and "feminine". Also in the first study, during the sorting tasks and at the end of the tasks, the participants were given the opportunity to discuss their responses to the photographs. These responses generated a further 21 constructs for the current study, amounting to 87 UX constructs in total. In order to also include aspects of emotion and pleasure, which were discussed in the interviews, constructs such as *Exciting, Desirable, Pleasurable*, and *It feels good to touch*, were also included. Other constructs that were evident in the interviews were as follows: *Good specifications, I would recommend it, Mysterious, Understandable, Exciting, I need this device, Useful, Can access its functionality easily, Reminds me of something else, I can understand it, It all fits together well, I can find my way around it, Lots to explore, I am curious about it, It is curious, I connect it with my sense of self, Interesting, Desirable, It feels good to hold, It feels good to carry, Nothing special*. The final questionnaire with the constructs for rating is shown in Appendix-B.

In order to select suitable devices for this study, the data from the previous study were used to derive four 'typical' MP3 players (Fig. 4.2). These were canonical examples from four device *categories* that emerged from the analysis of the way people conceptualised devices using 35 MP3 player photographs. Participants tended to distinguish the MP3 players initially in terms of their shape, colour and landscape/portrait orientation of their screens. The regions in the MSA plot from the study show four basic types of MP3 players: *Standard, Curved, Horizontal* and *Other*. For this study, participants were required to rate an example model from each category (circled in pink in Fig. 4.2). A condition of their recruitment was that they had not used that model before. This was a challenging criterion to fulfil in the case of the *iPod Classic* which was a canonical example of the 'standard' category in the first study, due to the ubiquity of this device amongst the participant demographic.

The inclusion of the *iPod Classic* in this study was an important decision to consider. To remove it from the study would be tantamount to ignoring a very significant aspect of media devices that were part of music-listening culture and technology. To keep it, would reduce the contrast of comparing photo-experience and physical-experience, for those who have had experience of it, even if it was a fleeting experience. However, since the *iPod Touch* was a recent arrival in the marketplace, it was easier to find model-naïve participants for it, instead of the *iPod Classic*. Therefore, the *iPod Touch* was substituted for the *iPod Classic* because it still matched the *iPod Classic's* shape, size and orientation. Both the *iPod Classic* and *iPod Touch* are roughly the same shape, they both have portrait orientation, and plain colour (black or white). This puts them in the same 'region'.

Fig. 4.3 Placement of *iPod Touch* (Device-2) in MSA from the initial study

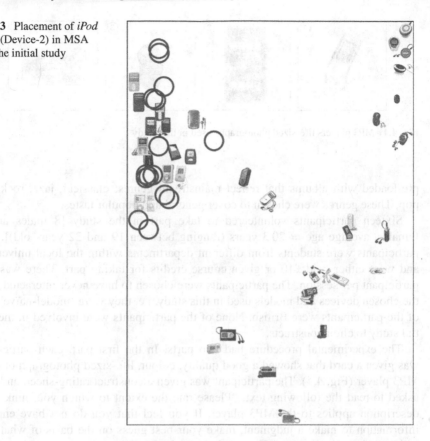

In order to test that the substitution of the *iPod Touch* was a valid one, 16 participants were individually shown a full-sized colour photograph of an *iPod Touch* and then asked to place a mark on the MSA plot from Study-1, where they thought the device would fit if it were part of the plot. The instructions were "Please place a mark where you think this device might be amongst this plot". Each pink circle shown in Fig. 4.3 shows the mark placed by one participant. From this plot, it can be clearly seen that there is overwhelming agreement that the *iPod Touch* is part of the same class as the *iPod Classic*. This result shows that using the *iPod Touch* instead of the *iPod Classic* is a valid substitution.

The *iPod Touch* also introduces a new paradigm of interaction with MP3 players, which makes it novel to prior users of the *iPod Classic*, where the touch aspect was not on the screen, but a separate surface control. Also, the controls on the *iPod Touch* are dynamic, in the sense that they change location and function according to context instead of being fixed physical buttons with a limited range of functionality. This introduces more complexity into the interaction aspect of the experience. The chosen MP3 player models for the study were therefore: iRiver (T-10), Apple (iPod Touch), Sony (Bean), Creative (MuVo-Slim). Each MP3 player was

Fig. 4.4 MP3 players life-sized photographs used in this study

pre-loaded with albums that reflect mainstream genres: classical, jazz, rock and pop. These genres were chosen to cover general and popular tastes.

Sixteen participants volunteered to take part in the study [8 males and 8 females, average age = 20.3 years (ranging between 19 and 22 years old)]. The participants were students from different departments within the local university, and were either paid £10 or given course credits for taking part. There was one participant per session. The participants were chosen to have never interacted with the chosen devices and models used in this study, i.e. they were 'model-naïve'. All of the participants were British. None of the participants were involved in the initial study to elicit constructs.

The experimental procedure had two parts. In the first part, each participant was given a card that showed a good quality, colour, life-sized photograph of each MP3 player (Fig. 4.4). The participant was given a construct rating-sheet, and was asked to read the following text: "Please rate the extent to which you think each description applies to the MP3 player. If you feel that you do not have enough information to make a judgment, make your best guess on the basis of what you see, and tick the box 'Not Enough Information'." Thus, participants were given the option of indicating that they were making a 'guess'. However, they were still required to rate according to what they 'saw' in the photograph, but information was recorded to indicate that they felt they did not have enough information to comfortably rate the construct in the rating-sheet. They were asked to indicate this feeling by placing a mark in a box labelled 'Not enough information'.

Once ratings were made from the photograph, the second part of the procedure was started, and it involved the participant being given the actual device that was represented in the photograph and they were informed of the different choices of music available on the MP3 player. The user manual was available for all devices. The participant was then asked to interact with it for a maximum duration of ten minutes as though they were playing with it in a shop or using a friend's device. The participants were not informed of the time limit. At the end of this period (which was as low as two minutes for some participants or as long as ten minutes for others), the participant was then given a new rating-sheet and asked to rate the actual device.

At the end of the second rating, the participant was then given the next MP3 player photograph in the list. This cycle was then repeated until all four MP3 players had been interacted with. In order to minimize order-effects, the devices were presented to the participants in the order dictated by a variant of a Latin square. In this order, no sequence was repeated among the 16 individual sessions.

At the beginning of each session with each device, each participant was asked to give a preference rating for the device (by viewing the photograph of the device), and then asked to give another preference rating once they had ended their physical interaction. The preference ratings were scored on a scale of 1–10, where 1 = low preference and 10 = high preference.

4.2.2 Super-Constructs

The results of this study are shown below in three sections: dynamics of super-constructs, device-specific results, and general results over all the devices.

In order to understand the underlying dimensions represented by the constructs, it was necessary to examine the overall way in which people apply them. Thus, by examining the correlations between the construct ratings, groups of constructs can be identified that are related to the same meaningful concepts. This was achieved by analysing the construct rating data using multidimensional scaling (MDS). In this way, the relationship between the constructs is represented in geometric space such that the correlation between each pair of constructs is inversely proportional to the distance between them. The MDS therefore provides a visual summary of the correlation matrix. In practice this means that two constructs that are applied in the same way, across all of the 64 samplings (16 participants multiplied by four MP3 players), will be plotted closer together in the space.

The MDS used here is Smallest Space Analysis (SSA) and the correlation co-efficient is Pearson's (Shye et al. 1994). The data were first examined in order to exclude any ratings that were highly skewed. Second, constructs were excluded where 30 % or more of the sample agreed that they did not have enough information to make the judgement. Finally, the coding for any constructs that carried a negative connotation were reversed, such that a rating of 1 became 7, 2 changed to a 6 and so on. This allows the meaning of the construct to be maintained over the directionality of the judgement. For constructs that were reverse coded, the word 'Not' will be used as a prefix, and flagged on the plot with an asterisk. For example, the construct is shown as '*Average', means 'Not Average', i.e. the rating for 'Average' reversed.

The results of the SSA are shown in Figs. 4.5 and 4.6, representing the construct ratings before and after interaction respectively. The Guttman-Lingoes' coefficient of alienation for these plots was 0.228 (before interaction) and 0.188 (after interaction) for a two dimensional solution, which indicates an accep level of fit (Shye et al. 1994, p. 125).

Figure 4.5 indicates the range of constructs rated with confidence from the photographs alone. The regions drawn on to the plots represent the researcher's interpretation of the structure of the plot. As with exploratory factor analysis, the researcher examines the groupings of constructs and forms an hypothesis as to

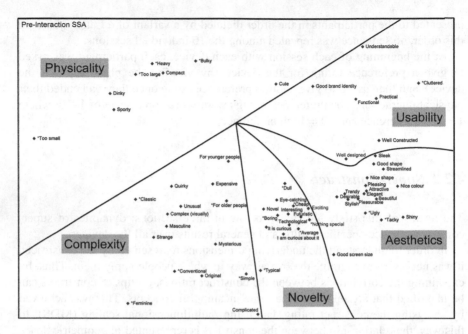

Fig. 4.5 Pre-interaction SSA plot showing the five similarity regions for the rating of anticipated experience with all players. The axes in this plot are related to the degree of correlation between points, and have no inherent dimension or orientation

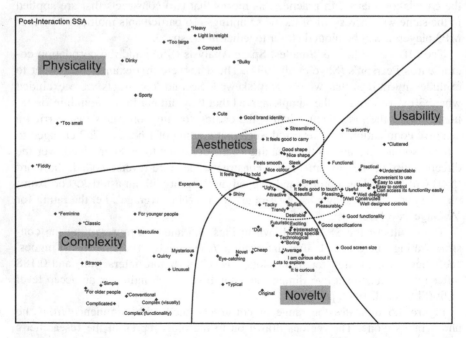

Fig. 4.6 Post-interaction SSA plot showing a change in the similarity regions for rating the actual experience with all players. The axes in this plot are related to the degree of correlation between points, and have no inherent dimension or orientation

their shared meaning. Five groups of constructs were identified that share a similarity in terms of their underlying meaning. These regions are proposed as the five dimensions of user experience: *Novelty, Usability, Complexity, Aesthetics* and *Physicality*. Although the same five dimensions are present in the before and after interaction plots the relationship between them is slightly different. In the pre-interaction SSA plot (Fig. 4.5), the five regions form a simple polarising facet indicative of five qualitatively different themes (Shye et al. 1994).

The region labelled 'Novelty' contains constructs such as *Novel, Not Typical*, and *Not Average*, as well as *Exciting, Not Boring* and *Not Nothing Special*. Also seen in this region are *Eye-catching, Interesting, Not Dull, I am curious about it*, and *It is curious*. Interestingly, participants also used the constructs *Futuristic* and *Technical* as part of the Novelty theme, as well as *Not Cheap*.

The region labelled 'Complexity' contains a set of related constructs including *Complicated, Complex (Visually), Not Simple, Original, Unusual, Not Conventional, Strange, Quirky, Not Classic* and *Mysterious*. Whilst *Expensive* is found in this region it is close to the border with 'Novelty' and therefore maybe used in a similar way to *Not cheap*. On the other hand, being 'cheap' may contain a set of connotations that go beyond the actual price. It is interesting that the age and gender related constructs correlate most highly with 'Complexity', i.e. *For younger people, Not For older people, Masculine* and *Not Feminine*. It seems that Complexity is associated with young males.

The region described as 'Physicality' relates to the 'mass' and 'size' of the device, in other words the substance of the device. The constructs found in this region are *Not Heavy, Not Bulky, Not Too large, Not Too small*. Also related to the device's physicality are *Compact* and *Sporty*, as well as *Dinky* and *Cute*.

'Usability' is a well-known and understood topic, defined as "the extent to which a product can be used by specified users to achieve specified goals with effectiveness, efficiency and satisfaction in a specified context of use." (ISO-9241-11 1998). Also, according to Nielson, Usability is related to Learnability, Efficiency, Memorability and Satisfaction (Nielson 1994). These aspects of the definition can therefore be seen in the group of constructs that include *Practical, Functional, Not Cluttered* and *Understandable*, as well as *Well designed* and *Well constructed*. Interestingly, *Good brand-identity* is also found here. Most of the constructs that were categorised as 'not enough information' where in the Usability region in the pre-Interaction SSA.

The final region is labelled 'Aesthetics' and contains constructs relating to form and evaluation, including *Good shape, Nice shape, Streamlined, Sleek* and *Elegant* as well as *Beautiful, Attractive, Pleasing, Desirable, Pleasurable, Shiny, Nice colour, Not Tacky, Trendy, Not Ugly* and *Stylish*.

The post-interaction SSA plot in Fig. 4.6 shows a carry-over of the same five regions found in the pre-interaction plot of Fig. 4.5 with some small alterations in the specific construct locations. *Usability, Novelty, Physicality* and *Complexity* are represented as four qualitatively different regions in the same polar structure as pre-interaction. More constructs are visible in these regions after interaction, because the participants felt able to rate certain constructs that they previously could not.

Usability in particular gains better definition with the addition of *Usable, Easy to control, Useful, Convenient to use, Easy to use, Can access its functionality easily, Well designed controls, Good screen size* and *It feels good to touch.*

However, the most interesting difference in the structure of the post interaction SSA is that the group of constructs that formerly represented *Aesthetics* as a separate region are now represented in the centre of the plot such that *Aesthetics* is a subset of all of the other dimensions, i.e. forms a 'core' group of constructs with associations not only to each other but with some relationship to all of the other dimensions of experience.

In the post-interaction SSA plot, the Aesthetics group of constructs were related to the physical nature of the device, e.g. *Well constructed, Feels smooth, It feels good to touch, It feels good to hold, It feels good to carry,* and even *Cute.* There were also constructs that were related to the evaluative aspects of Complexity e.g. *Expensive, Futuristic* and *Exciting.* Finally, there were constructs that reflected an overall evaluative nature e.g. *Trustworthy* and *Good brand identity.*

One of the ways that SSA plots are used, is to derive 'themes' of constructs that are empirically related to each other. The constructs on the SSA plot that are close together, by definition, are highly correlated. Therefore, they would yield a high Cronbach's Alpha score. This means that if these constructs were to be used to measure the theme, then they would be a good measure of that theme. Each region of the SSA plot can therefore be conceived of as a scale of UX.

4.2.3 Developing UX-Scales

The post interaction SSA plot in the Study-2 provided a source of dimensions of UX. Each region contributed a number of constructs that belonged to a general theme: *Novelty, Usability, Complexity, Aesthetics* and *Physicality* (Appendix D). Using the constructs in each region (or theme) as items in a scale, the scales were tested for reliability using Cronbach's Alpha, and were found to have high scores in Table 4.2.

Each of the constructs within each scale can be converted for use on the questionnaire. While most constructs could be used as they were, a few may need slight alteration. For example 'masculine' could be converted to 'looks masculine'. The new list of constructs was then used to form a rating scale. Each item could be

Table 4.2 Cronbach's Alpha scale reliability scores for the five super-constructs

Scale	Cronbach's alpha	No. of items
Novelty	0.943	11
Usability	0.955	18
Complexity	0.864	11
Aesthetics	0.949	25
Physicality	0.895	16

listed against a 7-point Likert scale, which could be shown, for example, to range between 'very unimportant' (1), to 'very important' (7). The rating sheet could be accompanied by simple instructions: "Regarding this device, please rate the extent to which you think each item in the list is important to YOU, right NOW, NOT whether it is good or bad, but whether it is something that is worth paying attention to." Analysing the data for average rating for each super-construct group, would then give a relative numerical value for each of the constructs.

In summary then, the SSA analysis has revealed five dimensions of UX derived from empirical analysis of people's ratings of mobile media devices. These five dimensions are defined by their construct content that can be used to form a reliable measurement instrument for future studies.

4.2.4 Construct Stability and Volatility

The SSA plots provided access to the way participants, as a group, experienced photographs and then the physical devices. However, the SSA plots do not show how these experiences varied at a device-level, nor at the level of the individual participants. However, the data in this study do hold this information, and analysing the data in a different way can therefore yield this extra insight. Therefore, to understand experiences at these levels, the changes in each of the ratings must be examined, as well as the qualitative data. In this way more of the *personal* nature of constructs may be illuminated, as well as aspects related to the individual devices.

In order to enhance the understanding of the changes in user experience from a qualitative point of view, extracts from the interview data were obtained during the rating tasks and the post-rating interviews. These verbal comments reveal device-specific accounts of the participants' experiences and complement the device-independent analysis presented above. In particular they show that although the overall construction of aesthetics changed to become more holistic with experience, individual device perceptions were subject to both positive or negative change, depending on whether they satisfied or contradicted initial expectations. Although both qualitative and quantitative analyses has been published elsewhere (Al-Azzawi et al. 2010b), it is useful to summarise the findings regarding construct stability.

The data were also analysed from a construct point of view in order to explore overall rating changes. In this way, the changes in the ratings would be examined in the context of constructs that may or may not be susceptible to change in ratings after interaction takes place, regardless of direction of change. Therefore, absolute changes in mean rating (Z), rather than signed changes, would show constructs that are prone to change, regardless of which device. For example a rating of 4 that changes to a rating of 2, once interaction takes place, would yield a value of 2 for Z. The Z value for each construct was calculated for each individual participant (see Table 4.3 for an example). This was repeated for each device. Once these

Table 4.3 Example data for participant P-07 rating for the iRiver device-1. The delta (Z) column is the absolute difference between pre and post interaction rating values

No.	Construct	Pre	Post	Delta (Z)
1	Expensive	3	2	1
2	Heavy	2	1	1
3	Feminine	4	4	0
4	Average	5	5	0
5	Nice colour	2	4	2
6	Beautiful	2	3	1
7	Good screen size	2	2	0
8	Practical	2	4	2
9	Original	5	4	1

values had been obtained, the total frequency of different Z values for each construct was counted (e.g. how many times was there a Z value of 2 for the *Heavy* construct?)

The purpose of these Z values was to discount idiosyncratic effects, or changes due to individual differences. For example, if *Heavy* was a construct that was rated markedly higher by one participant after interaction, but was rated markedly lower by another participant, this would give an indication that *Heavy* is a construct that participants are likely to change their mind about. Conversely, if participants hardly changed their minds about the *Brand Identity* of a device, regardless of interaction, then the *Brand Identity* is a construct that resists change post-interaction. In this way, the constructs may be generalisable as interaction-sensitive or interaction-insensitive constructs.

A plot showing the distribution of the frequency of occurrence of the Z values was created for each construct (e.g. Fig. 4.7), and the skew and kurtosis were measured as a means of objectively characterising the distribution. Skew is a measure of 'bunching' of the distribution, where bunching on the left indicates a higher skew, and bunching to the right shows a lower skew. Kurtosis, however, is a measure of the peakedness (leptokurtic) or flatness (platykurtic) of a distribution.

These values would indicate if there was general agreement in how much the rating changed by (high kurtosis, leptokurtic), or a spread of responses (low kurtosis, platykurtic). Also, a high positive value for skew would indicate fewer changes in the ratings, i.e. mostly low Z values. Conversely, lower values of skew would indicate higher changes in ratings, i.e. higher Z values (Fig. 4.8). Table 4.4 shows the types of constructs that would most likely show a change in the rating once interaction takes place. They are also the constructs that exhibit the highest degree of diversity in the change in the ratings post-interaction. Therefore, these are the constructs that are the most volatile (bottom left in Fig. 4.8).

Conversely, the data in Table 4.5 show the types of constructs that are least likely to change after interaction, and show lower diversity in the amount of change in ratings, post interaction. Therefore, these more resilient constructs are the most s (top right in Fig. 4.8).

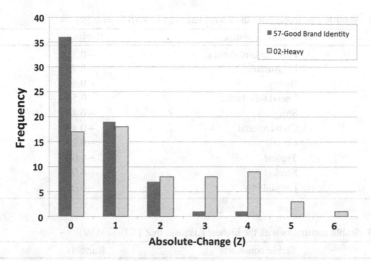

Fig. 4.7 Frequency plots of absolute-change in rating (Z), showing an example of: '*stable*' constructs with high count for Z values and Kurtosis (*Good Brand Identity*), and '*volatile*' constructs, showing a spread of counts for Z values and low Kurtosis (*Heavy*)

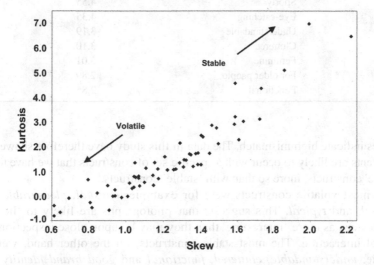

Fig. 4.8 Scatter plot for all the constructs used in this study, showing the spread between volatile and stable constructs

The mismatch between anticipated and actual experience may be reflected in the absolute change in ratings (Z values), where a user may have an idea of what to expect and then react: "oh! I thought it was…but it turned out …". This indicates a mismatch between anticipated and actual perceived experience, which was also found by Swallow et al., where they concluded that *"there may be a large gap between the expectations generated by marketing and the actual experiences in practice of representative users"* (Swallow et al. 2005, p. 98). In this case, high

Table 4.4   Volatile constructs with the lowest Kurtosis in Z (S.E. = 0.59)

No.	Volatile constructs	Kurtosis
79	I am curious about it	−0.81
88	Pleasurable	−0.75
2	Heavy	−0.66
64	I need this device	−0.58
34	Shiny	−0.48
30	Conventional	−0.40
22	Classic	−0.28
67	Typical	−0.09
31	Sleek	−0.06
36	I would buy	−0.02

Table 4.5   Stable constructs with the highest Kurtosis in Z (S.E. = 0.59)

No.	Stable constructs	Kurtosis
51	Streamlined	6.97
57	Good brand identity	6.47
42	For younger people	5.08
46	Sporty	4.55
26	Eye-catching	4.35
62	Understandable	3.19
59	Cluttered	3.10
3	Feminine	3.01
14	For older people	2.89
21	Functional	2.85

Z values indicate high mismatch. The data in this study have therefore showed that such events are likely to occur with a specific set of constructs that we have termed 'volatile' constructs, more so than with 'stable' constructs.

The most volatile constructs were for example: *unusual, pleasurable, conventional*, and *typical*. This suggests that photographs are likely to 'lie', and show devices as more 'interesting' than they may be upon close inspection after physical interaction. The most stable constructs, on the other hand, were for example: *understandable, cluttered, functional* and *good brand identity*. This suggests that users are not likely to change their minds about aspects related to usability and brand. It is interesting that good brand identity is one of the most s of all constructs. This gives more credence to the idea that people are less likely to change their mind about the brand aspect of a device, based on one iteration or cycle of interaction. This is not to say that s constructs are not evaluative (e.g. leading to like or dislike decisions), it is just that the evaluation tends to be resilient to change post-interaction, whereas volatile constructs are susceptible to change through use. Essentially, participants would have already had their anticipations with the photo-rating session, regarding the stable constructs, and the interaction did not give them a mismatch. Conversely, for volatile constructs, their anticipations brought to the photo-session were 'erroneous', and led to subsequently feeling a mismatch during actual interaction. Such reconstruing could eventually lead to emotional evaluative responses, to disenchantment, or enchantment for being pleasantly surprised (McCarthy et al. 2006).

In this study, the knowledge and anticipations that the participants brought to the study are considered part of the evolving user experience and evaluations. These anticipations were then exposed in the form of ratings. This knowledge that is brought to an event is modified upon subsequent visual (image) and physical interactions with the next physical device, a similar device or any other. Importantly however, all previous knowledge being brought to an event, including the 'lack-of-knowledge', i.e. what they do not know is part of their general anticipation. Therefore, volatility is an indication of a susceptibility to change, and is a dimension of a construct, with Volatile and Stable being the two poles of the dimension. Volatility is therefore related to the mismatch between anticipated and actual experiences.

Hassenzahl suggested that ratings and preferences were related to the type of construct: hedonic or pragmatic. In his second study, using virtual interactive products, he showed that "pragmatic attributes as well as goodness were affected by experience (i.e. usability problems), whereas hedonic attributes and beauty remained stable over time" (Hassenzahl 2004, p. 340). Hassenzahl (2004, p. 339) refers to the increase in mental effort as a primary cause of the change in usability ratings. Importantly, the real and physical aspects of interaction were missing from that study, and the data in this research show that aesthetics (e.g. *Classic* and *Sleek*) and physicality (e.g. *Heavy*) constructs are amongst the most volatile constructs, suggesting that mismatch can occur with both, 'pragmatic' as well as 'hedonic' aspects of interaction.

4.3 Summary

The studies were conducted in order to explore the changes in aspects of User Experience during the early stages of first-time interaction, and to investigate possible classification of constructs, in order to further understand UX. The data have allowed the classification of constructs into five super-constructs, or five dimensions of UX: *Novelty*, *Usability*, *Complexity*, *Aesthetics* and *Physicality*.

The data in these studies have also demonstrated idiosyncratic behaviour, emphasising the personal nature of 'personal' constructs, as well as anticipation being a significant aspect of user experience. There were also demonstrations of two general types of constructs. Ones that are more *s* and are resistant to change after interaction takes place, as well as ones that are more *volatile* and are more prone to change. The data also show how physical aspects play an important role in UX. Brand also played an important role, where it influenced the *resilience* of ratings to change, as well as showing overwhelming positive influence on ratings for more prominent brands that already have a positive reputation.

The above findings now raise questions about longer-term experiences such as consumption, and the way the importance of the five dimensions of UX (5D-UX) change over long periods, and whether some are more important than others. And also questions about how these changes may be quantifiable.

References

Kelly, G. A. (1955). *The psychology of personal constructs, Volume One: Theory and personality* (1991 edn. Vol. 1). London: Routledge.

Hassenzahl, M. (2004). The interplay of beauty, goodness, and usability in interactive products. *Human-Computer Interactions, 19*, 319–349.

Frohlich, D. (2004). Beauty as a design prize. *Human-Computer Interaction, 19*, 359–366.

Norman, D. A. (2004). Introduction to this special section on beauty, goodness, and usability. *Human-Computer Interaction, 19*, 311–318.

Hassenzahl, M., Burmester, M., & Koller, F. (2003). AttrakDiff: Ein Fragebogen zur Messung wahrgenommener hedonischer und pragmatischer Qualität (AttracDiff: A questionnaire to measure perceived hedonic and pragmatic quality). In J. Ziegler & G. Szwillus (Eds.), *Mensch & Computer 2003. Interaktion in Bewegung* (pp. 187–196). Stutgart, Leipzig: B. G. Teubner.

Al-Azzawi, A., Frohlich, D., & Wilson, M. (2007). Beauty constructs for MP3 players. *CoDesign—International Journal of CoCreation in Design and the Arts, Affective Communication in Design—Challenges for Researchers* (3-S1), 59–74.

Canter, D., Brown, J., & Groat, L. (1985). A multiple sorting procedure. In M. Brenner, J. Brown, & D. Canter (Eds.), *The research interview: Uses and approaches*. London: Academic Press.

Wilson, M. (1995). Structuring qualitative data: Multidimensional scalogram analysis. In G. Breakwell, S. Hammond, & C. Fife-Shaw (Eds.), *Research methods in psychology*. London: Sage Publications.

Zvulun, E. (1978). Multidimensional scalogram analysis: The method and its application. In S. Shye (Ed.), *Theory construction and data analysis in the behavioural science*. San Francisco: Jossey-Bass.

Wilson, M. (1996). The socialization of architectural preferences. *Journal of Environmental Psychology, 16*, 33–44.

Tractinsky, N., Shoval-Katz, A., & Ikar, D. (2000). What is beautiful is usable. *Interacting with Computers, 13*, 127–145.

Logan, R. J., Augaitis, S. R., & Renk, T. (1994). *Design of simplified television remote controls: A case for behavioral and emotional usability.* Paper presented at the Human Factors and Ergonomics Society 38th Annual Meeting, Santa Monica, CA.

Hassenzahl, M., & Tractinsky, N. (2006). User experience-a research agenda. *Behaviour & Information Technology, 25*(2), 91–97.

Mahlke, S. (2006). *Aesthetic and Symbolic Qualities as Antecedents of Overall Judgements of Interactive Products.* Paper presented at the People and Computers XX–Engage: HCI 2006, London.

Minge, M. (2008). *Dynamics of user experience.* Paper presented at the Research Goals and Strategies for Studying User Experience and Emotion—NordiCHI2008, Lund, Sweden.

Thüring, M., & Mahlke, S. (2007). Usability, aesthetics, and emotions in human-technology-interaction. *International Journal of Psychology, 42*, 253–264.

Shye, S., Elizur, D., & Hoffman, M. (1994). *Introduction to facet theory*. Thousand Oaks: Sage.

Nielson, J. (1994). *Usability engineering (Interactive technologies)*. San Francisco: Morgan Kaufmann.

Al-Azzawi, A., Frohlich, D., & Wilson, M. (2010b). *Stability of user experience: Changes in constructs as users transition from anticipated to actualised interaction*. Paper presented at the iHCI 2010, Dublin.

Swallow, D., Blyth, M. A., & Wright, P. C. (2005). *Grounding experience: Relating theory and method to evaluate the user experience of smartphones*. Paper presented at the Proceedings of the 2005 annual conference on European association of cognitive ergonomics.

McCarthy, J., Wright, P. C., Wallace, J., & Dearden, A. (2006). The experience of enchantment in human-computer interaction. *Personal and Ubiquitous Computing, 10*(6), 369–378.

Chapter 5
Construct Dynamics: Consumption

Abstract With regards to long-term dynamics, this chapter proposes consumption as a 'frame' for experience, and the Consumer Decision Process (CDP) is suggested as a useful analogue for the experience cycle. The CDP is subsequently simplified to a sequence of four phases, ABCD: *Approach*, *Buying*, *Consummation*, and *Divestment* which forms the basis of a case-study. Essentially, the case-study involves conducting interview surveys to assess the long- term user experience of 16 participants who are traversing these phases, tracking the individual participants at the junctures *immediately before*, *immediately after*, and *sometime after* their acquisition of a mobile media device. The aim of the study is to find qualitative themes and super-constructs to enrich the ICE model and to augment the findings from previous studies. Relationships are found to exist between object and participant, and with others; the issue of brand is particularly emphasised. Finally, the interviews which took place with one participant are used to explore a cohesive and connected experience, where the data also highlight the notion of 'implications'. This supports the idea that experience can be described as an interaction between personal, physical and social contexts.

Keywords Consumption • Self • Brand • Relationships • Implications • Human–Computer interaction (HCI) • Mobile device usability • Phenomenology • User experience (UX) • User experience dynamics

5.1 Scaling Experience

In order to get a sense of the changes in how people experience technology, previous research has used physical time as a scale to measure the changes in these experiences as time passes in seconds (Lindgaard et al. 2006), minutes (Hassenzahl 2004; Minge 2008; Thüring and Mahlke 2007; Tractinsky et al. 2000), hours (Vyas and van der Veer 2006), days (Swallow et al. 2005), weeks (Karapanos et al. 2009), as well as years (von Wilamowitz-Moellendorff et al. 2006). These studies measure user experience pre-, during- and post-interaction at different intervals of real-time. On the other

A. al-Azzawi, *Experience with Technology*, SpringerBriefs in Computer Science, DOI: 10.1007/978-1-4471-5397-9_5, © The Author(s) 2014

hand, others, like McCarthy and Wright (2004), measure experience through case-studies that examine sense-making processes and the "threads of experience". Their framework is neither sequential nor linear, which distances it from physical time, therefore not an ordinal structure, i.e. there is no temporal order to the framework. This makes it difficult to relate to the chronological order of the case study, however, the processes they describe are nonetheless on-going for the user, throughout use. They specifically point out that the processes that people use to make sense, e.g. *appropriation* or *recounting*, are "ideas" that help researchers and designers by describing and understanding the user experience. In one case study (2004, p. 131), they illustrate the journey of an e-commerce shopper and his buying experience. Therefore, by necessity, the journey is chronological. However, they focus their attention on highlighting the areas that show such processes as *anticipations* and first-impressions, as well as *reflecting* on the on-going experience, including the "threads of experience", such as the sensual descriptions on the web site. In this way McCarthy and Wright describe a consumer's journey in 'meaningful time', i.e. how the user was making meaning as time went on, rather than describing the business phases of consumption (e.g. marketing, purchase, after-sales). They also described how the user related to the supplier, the manufacturer, as well as others in his life, including friends and family as well as the artifacts themselves, e.g. the web site, and computers.

The above apparent discrepancy between physical and psychological time poses a dilemma in terms measuring the dynamics of UX. However, as shown earlier, meaning and sense making are fundamental aspects of experience, and the constant re-construing process that Kelly (1955) refers to, implicitly and explicitly shows cyclical changes in the meaning. In the 'experience corollary' of his PCT, Kelly explains that the sense of looking ahead, and bringing previous experiences to bear on new upcoming experiences is a key aspect of experience. As Kelly puts it, experience has units or quanta: "The unit of experience is, therefore, a cycle embracing five phases: anticipation, investment, encounter, confirmation or disconfirmation, and constructive revisions" (Kelly 2003, p. 12).

In the above description of a single cycle of experience, Kelly describes anticipation as the starting phase, where a person approaches the artifact with the backdrop of their past experiences and a sense of expectation of what they are about to discover. Next, he describes 'investment' that is the amount of effort a person will put into the situation. The more a person invests in a situation, i.e. the more they are involved, the more experience they have. Encounter is the point where consummation of the anticipations occurs, i.e. the person encounters the artifact, in actual use. The next phase is where the person's anticipations are either confirmed or not, or a mixture of the two. Finally, the person reconstrues, in order to develop a new understanding, which is now dependent on the way they have understood the new 'evidence'. In this way, Kelly has described the rudimentary phases in meaning making, and provides a chronological way to measure meaningful experience.

This model is very close to the classification proposed by Arnould et al. (2004), p. 347, where consumer experiences are classified into four types: *anticipated consumption, purchase experience, consumption experience* and *remembered consumption and nostalgia*. The anticipation and remembered aspects of the consumption experience are also reflected in McCarthy and Wright's (2004) model of experience with technology, discussed earlier, although they do not specifically describe it as a cyclical relationship as such. This classification of 'consumption as experience' was first suggested by Holbrook and Hirschman (1982), which was later elaborated by Holt (1995). By experiential, they mean aspects such as "aesthetics... multisensory aspects of product enjoyment... syntactic dimensions [meaning]... pleasure... fantasies... feelings... play" (Holbrook and Hirschman 1982, p. 139). Carù and Cova (2007) emphasise that 'experience' itself is the target of consumption. Holbrook and Hirschman make the point that this experiential perspective "is phenomenological in spirit and regards consumption as a primarily subjective state of consciousness with a variety of symbolic meanings, hedonic responses, and aesthetic criteria" (1982, p. 132). These 'states' are clearly related to the description of user experience discussed in Chaps. 2 and 3. This makes consumption, and its related phases and cycles, useful 'frames' for exploring experience.

In other words, consumption may be seen as an exemplar of an 'experience cycle', both in terms of the Holbrook and Hirschman's view of 'consumption as experience' (above), and the cyclical classification described by Arnould et al. (above), as well as Kelly's reference to the "unit of experience" (above). Combining these three points of view makes it possible to use consumption as a 'frame' to explore UX. Indeed, Andrews et al. used the view of 'consumption as experience' to explore the emotional aspects of mobile phone use (Andrews et al. 2005). Another view of the above as explicitly a cycle is the 'Buying Process' (Foxall and Goldsmith 1994, p. 26), having four stages: *Want/Need Development*, *Pre-Purchase Planning & Decision*, *Purchase*, and *Post-Purchase & Evaluation*. Doblin's framework of 'Compelling Experience' shows a strikingly similar view (See Kumar 2013, p. 178), and, as part of a holistic, systems-thinking approach, Norman (2009) highlights *discovery*, *purchase* and *anticipation* of use, as significant aspects of the whole user experience.

5.2 Consumption as a Scale

Kelly's description of the experience cycle, as well as the other cycles described above, are similar to the phases of consumption. However, although consumption is presented in this section as a detailed description of the stages that people follow when consuming products, it is important to note that this is a generalisation. Consumers behave differently when planning to purchase a large-item, when buying out of habit or when buying at the checkout due to an impulsive reaction (see Solomon et al. 2006, p. 324). Such a framework may nonetheless provide access to how people experience technology. This is not to say that all technology experience is through the process of consumption, or even choice. However, since the focus for this research is on mobile digital media products, the assumption is that users are also 'consumers'. Therefore, a useful scale of meaningful relationships between people and objects is that of the relationship between consumers and consumer products, where such a scale may be operationalised in a research project.

The consumption of products has been described in the marketing and business literature as a serial process of activities that consumers engage in. Even though other models are very similar (Howard and Sheth 1969; Nicosia 1966), the most prominent model is that of Engel et al. (1968). This model is called the Consumer Decision Process (CDP) and has its roots with Dewey's earlier model of "How we think" (1910). However, the CDP has been criticised for stressing the decision making aspects, and not giving the anticipatory elements of consumption enough emphasis (Pham 1995). Nonetheless, the CDP is intended to provide a "road map of consumers' minds that marketers and managers can use to help guide product mix, communication and sales strategies" (Blackwell et al. 2006, p. 70). Therefore, it is the "consumers minds" that are of interest in this book.

The seven steps in the CDP model are: *need recognition, search for information, pre-purchase evaluation, purchase, consumption, post-purchase evaluation,* and *divestment.* The steps in the CDP are described as being influenced by two main factors: *environmental influences* and *individual differences* (Blackwell et al. 2006). For environmental influences, there are such factors as: Social class, Culture, Family, Personal influences, and Situation (also highlighted by Mehrabian and Russell 1974, p. 8). However, for individual differences, influential factors are: consumer resources (e.g. finance or time), motivation (e.g. urgency), knowledge, attitudes, personality, values (e.g. fun or practicality), and lifestyle (Blackwell et al. 2006, p. 70). The main psychological influences on the CDP are: information processing, learning and attitude & behaviour (Blackwell et al. 2006, p. 88). Information processing is related to how information is retrieved, transformed and stored. Learning, through marketing and actual use, is seen as the process by which experience influences knowledge, attitudes, and ultimately, behaviour.

The CDP described above is perhaps useful for the general case of consumption, but there have been other variants and applications [e.g. 'Innovation' by Rogers (2003), and 'professional services' by Barnes (Barnes 1986)]. To follow such specialist applications of the CDP, it may be fruitful to re-consider the generic CDP for the consumption of technological products, in particular, handheld media devices. For example, conceptual complexity or the notion of compatibility may be more relevant for such consumption. In this way, consumers may think of their existing products (e.g. accessories, or related software), when it comes to evaluating other products, pre- and post-purchase. However, when considering consumption of technology, it is important to also consider the cultural and contextual aspects of consumption, which form the prelude and preamble to the consuming experience, as well as anticipated use. The influence that culture imposes on technology is a well-researched topic, and in fact technology can be seen as a product of competing influences in society, e.g. the *Social Construction of Technology,* where the technology is 'shaped' and 'constructed' by the pressures of society, politics, and consumer behaviour (Pinch and Bijker 1987). The basic premise of this theory is that the very act of consumption is a major force that can shape the direction that technology evolves. Therefore, the consumer is an active 'actor' in the consumption process, and not merely a recipient of whatever the market 'offers' for consumption.

Consequently, with the emphasis on technology, the CDP may be described in the following seven phases, showing the *interactional, constructional,* and *evaluative* aspects (ICE) of the experiences within each phase:

1. **Need/Want**: The development of a need or want
2. **Exposure**: Gaining knowledge of innovations and exposure to products
3. **Choice**: Choosing a product according to preference criteria
4. **Purchase**: The decision to buy
5. **Use**: Actual consumption and implementation of the technology
6. **Retrospection**: Stories, narratives and confirmation of expectations
7. **Divestment**: Dissolution, discard or disuse after failure or satisfying the need.

Need/Want Development stage is one when people sense or develop a need where the technology is seen as a way to satisfy this need. The need could be for a socially desirable object, where owning (or 'displaying') such a device may influence their social standing amongst their peer-group (Bourdieu 1984). Although the CDP emphasises a need "recognition", it could be argued that for technology, it is more of a 'development', as described in the buying process. This nuance recognises the fact that there is a selling process that the consumer is taking part in, and part of the sales process is to help consumers develop the idea that they need a particular product. Technology may therefore be a need that is nurtured and developed by marketing efforts, targeting basic human needs (Maslow 1987).

Exposure or the *active and passive search for knowledge,* is about being aware of the technology or innovation itself, for example being aware that there are such things as devices that play a personal music collection on the move, in a convenient package that is compact and accessible. This awareness can have internal and external sources, i.e. knowledge already internalised and acquired over a long period of time from the environment, as well as knowledge gained explicitly by active searching. The length of search or exposure can vary and is dependent on many factors e.g. personality (Blackwell et al. 2006).

Choice and Persuasion is regarding the process of choosing from the available products and specifications. Preference criteria play an important role in this phase. Consumers will generally run though scenarios of how the different choices and attributes of products will fit into their lives, where they may ask questions like "what if…?" regarding the suitability of a 'really new product' (Hoeffler 2003). Consumers may have pre-formed criteria or factors that will influence their choices, such as price or brand. In particular, for technological products, they may pay special attention to the issue of technical compatibility, of what they are consuming, with the rest of the technical environment relevant to their consumption (e.g. audio file-formats), which may have impacted convenience. However, in-tangible aspects of technology also play a role in decision-making, e.g. the conceptual model or operation of a devices a user is exposed to is also important in this regard. Products manufacturers can follow standard models of operation, e.g. design patterns, to maintain high learnability for a new interaction models (Nielson 1994). However, purchasing decisions may be dominated by many effects, e.g. affect more than cognition (Zajonc and Markus 1982), or logical instead of being influenced by affective attributes (Christopher et al. 2003), or deciding based on 'cues' (Cue Utilisation Theory) (Hansen 2005). These factors (e.g. affect, cognition, cues etc.) may form a "hierarchy of effects" system that combine to influence consumer behaviour (Mowen 1988).

Purchase or acquisition point in the CDP is a pivotal point in the sense that a commitment has been made. Prior to this point, the consumer is free to think of options, while after this stage, the focus is about the product that has been chosen. Such decisions could be swayed by a sales promotion, shop opening-time, physical access, delivery time etc. (Blackwell et al. 2006). Critically, this phase represents a shift in power between the user and the supplier. Before purchase (*intended consumption*), the user was 'in control', making choices and being courted by the supplier, whereas after purchase (*actualised consumption*), the user has committed, and is on the receiving end in terms of any aftersales relationships with the supplier or manufacturer.

Use and Consumption stage in the CDP is where the user actually starts to *use* the device in order to fulfil the need that was developed or recognised earlier, taking possession of the device and having immediate or prolonged use. At this point, the user is required to operate the device, drawing on their existing knowledge to interpret controls, levers and buttons, as well as interpreting symbols. There is potential for errors that may influence emotional responses, where simple tasks may become complex, due to ambiguity.

Retrospection is about how the device fits in the whole narrative of the user's life and confirmation of expectations, or otherwise. This phase includes retrospective and remembered experiences, e.g. recalling a difficult time finding a suitable battery charger. Discrepancy between expectations and actual events contribute to satisfaction and dissatisfaction. So, a user may feel good about their expectations being met or exceeded or feel let down and disenchanted if their expectations are not met. Such recounting of experience and reflecting on decisions and behaviour, is also a means of making sense of the experience (McCarthy and Wright 2004), and appropriating such experiences as part of their narrative of the consumption process.

Dissolution and Divestment is the final phase in the CDP, where the product will come to the end of its life. There are many reasons why this could happen (Fajer and Schouten 1995). A simple reason is that it could fail or malfunction and require repair or recycling. Also, a product could come to a point where it no longer fulfils the need that was developed originally, or a sense of disenfranchisement or disenchantment, when a product no longer meets expectations and anticipated experience. The expectancy disconfirmation model explains such behaviour when a consumer is unable to confirm what they were expecting from the consumption (see Solomon et al. 2006, p. 329). Whichever the reason, the product will not be used any more, and it could be disposed of, sold, or spend the rest of its life in a top drawer.

5.3 Simplified Consumption

The above has been concerned with presenting a framework that is useful to describe the dynamics of User Experience in such a way that makes it possible to measure it. Consumption was used as such a frame, where it is viewed 'as experience' (Holbrook and Hirschman 1982). Kelly's description of a 'unit of experience' (2003, p. 12) was shown to fit well with the CDP approach. In this way consume-time is more useful than physical-time, where *time* is a construct that provides a basis for the sequential description of events. Therefore, the narrative or sense making processes may be accessed using such a framework. To this end, the Consumer Decision Process (CDP) was presented, pointing out particular points of interest that are specific to technological products, as well as highlighting the two distinct phases of consumption: *intended* and *actualised*, where construction and interaction occur heterogeneously. Intended consumption is dominated by sampled interaction (trying out devices) and figuring out options, and constructing meaning from device attributes and building expectations. This stage therefore has the least physical interaction, and is more of a constructive and anticipatory phase. Actualised consumption, on the other hand, is dominated by a lot of interactional activity, in the sense that there is more physical interaction taking place with the artifact and associated network of artifacts. This increased use or consummation, then turns into a mixture of interaction and construction of the meaning and evaluation of the interaction.

However, taking into account that the above phases in the CDP do not represent hard limits and boundaries, and in fact they tend to merge across each other, and a user may be in more than one at the same time, for different artifacts. It is therefore possible to group the seven CDP phases into four broader stages of focus in terms of exploring the dynamics of UX (Fig. 5.1). The first is *Approach*, which encompasses the first two phases, 'Need/Want' and 'Exposure'. The second stage is *Buying*, which is the pre- and post-acquisition, spanning 'Choice', 'Purchase' and 'Use'. The third stage is *Consummation* (or use), which includes 'Use' and 'Retrospection'. The final stage is *Dissolution and Divestment*, which is also the final phase of the CDP, i.e. 'Divestment'. These four stages are referenced by the acronym, *ABCD*, and form a simplified version of the CDP presented above. Both versions help contribute towards a refinement of the third research question. Instead of asking about the general change of UX in time, it is now possible to relate the question to how UX changes with respect to the above stages of consumption, ABCD.

5.4 Construct Dynamics During Consumption (Case-Study 3)

Although the previous studies provided insights into the way users experienced media devices over a variety of time-scales, in terms of long-term connected experiences, the data were lacking an in-depth understanding of users' experiences. Such experiences could be explored for themes that could be used to further enrich this research. Although, Study-2 did provide some qualitative data, those data were specifically collected to compare pre- and post-interaction, not general consumption. Though consumption itself is not of interest in this research per se, it nonetheless provides a useful framework that mimics experience cycles. Exploring the case-study in this section therefore aims to enrich the previous case-studies by

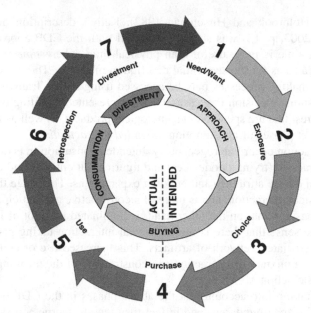

Fig. 5.1 Phases of the CDP, and consumption phases ABCD

exploring data from the interview-survey method, across the whole consumption cycle, in order to gain qualitative answers towards all three research questions: how users make meaning through their experience with technology, the nature of constructs of UX, and the dynamics of UX through consumption of technology.

Swallow et al. (2005) have already conducted a qualitative study to explore the user experience of Smartphones. They followed three participants through the use of a Smartphone on loan to them for the three-week duration of the study. The participants were asked to make voice-notes using the Smartphone, to reflect their experiences with it. The researchers then used *Grounded Theory* methodology to derive themes from voice-note data, and concluded with a proposed model of people's user experience with Smartphones. The result of their study suggested five themes: *identity, sociability, security* and *organisation*, with *relevance* as an underlying aspect (discussed earlier). In the way the authors describe their findings, the sociability and organisation themes were specific to the Smartphone, and may or may not generalise to experience with other technology such as MP3 players. Also, as the researchers point out in their results, some participants questioned the relevance of the Smartphone to their lives "whose opinions … seemed to hang on whether or not the device was appropriate to them" (Swallow et al. 2005, p. 96), and this could raise questions regarding the external validity of the data. This kind of issue could have been avoided if the study was centred on exploring participants' consumption experiences with their own devices. However, Karapanos et al. (2009) did exactly that, when they followed the experiences of people as they bought a Smartphone. Their way of exploring UX during consumption was to ask participant to record their experiences in the form of 'experience samples' (Day

Reconstruction Method) (discussed in Chap. 3). This method allowed participants to record a summary of their experiences at the end of the day, or the beginning of the next day, and rate their experience using an instrument with pre-conceived constructs. Unfortunately, their study was therefore predominately a quantitative study that was based on a priori theory of the constructs present in the data, thereby impeding the discovery of users' own constructs.

In contrast to the above studies, Vyas and van der Veer (2006) sought to follow users' experiences in the manner of: *pre-*, *during-*, and *post-interaction*. They did this with eleven participants using IPTV technology (discussed earlier). The advantages of their study is the acknowledgment of the phenomenological, constructive, and holistic nature of UX, and therefore ensuring their procedures and methods accounted for these aspects. They concluded with a recognition of the importance of *brand*, and *usability* as factors that influenced the participants' experiences. However, they had also used pre-defined lists of constructs as a way to explore UX with participants, rather than use open or semi-structured interviews. Importantly, their data was anchored in technology that is non-personal and not mobile.

The previous case-studies in this book have shown the sense of self to be both implicitly and explicitly important in the way participants expressed their experiences. Therefore, in order to facilitate a reasonable basis for comparison of data, and keep the same context and technology application (personal and mobile media players), the following case-study was chosen to maintain consistency with the previous case-studies presented here. Consequently, this case-study is discussed alongside the view that consumption is a cycle, just as experience can be seen as ever-present cycles. Therefore, in order to expand on the knowledge gained from study-2 for short-term experience cycles, the study presented here explores longer experience cycles in a qualitative longitudinal manner. The approach in this study is to treat the experience of consumption as phasic and holistic. Holistic in the sense that each phase makes sense in the presence of the other phases, not separate from them. The intention is therefore to find themes and constructs within consumption, especially ones that may have been undetectable in the methods in the earlier studies, and perhaps find further evidence of the earlier findings. To this end, this study is a collection of case studies of people who go through the process of buying an MP3 player. The interviews explore how these people think about their experiences when acquiring such devices, from the initial stages of consumption, right through and round again. The interviews were conducted at different phases of the CDP, in order to provide direct insight at these different phases. The simplified CDP (Fig. 5.1), ABCD, was then used to design the interview schedule (Appendix C).

It is important to note that there is no phase where a person would 'start' in the CDP. For example, at any one time, they are divesting something, that may be related to what they are about to use, or have just bought something that is similar (in some way) to what they are already using. However, the *Approach* phase seems a logical starting point because it marks a new relationship with a particular device. Therefore, *Approach* is the first phase. However, the time between the final two stages is unpredictable, and it could be as much as many years. Therefore, in the interest of being able ensure that data were collected at ALL the phases, for each of the participants, the interviews were started at the dissolution phase. This is methodologically valid since having the approach phase as the starting phase of the CDP is an arbitrary choice. Also, combining the dissolution phase from a previous device, with the approach of the new device, meant that that a minimum of three interviews were required. However, extra interviews were conducted where possible in order to collect more data. Therefore, the interviews were ordered as: *Dissolution & Approach, Buying* then *Consummation* (i.e. DABC).

5.4.1 Method

The study was completed with eight participants, with a mean age of 21 years (ranging between 18 and 26), all of which were university students (Table 5.1).

The participants volunteered after a general email request for users that were about to purchase an MP3 player. Participants were paid a small incentive upon completing the last interview. The following sections give a short description of the participants' profiles, using pseudonyms.

Casper (P-01) was involved in earlier pre and post-interaction study, and at that stage had little interest in MP3 players. During that study, he was introduced to an iPod Touch. He was so taken aback and smitten by the device, that he offered to buy it, which he later did as part of this study. This provided a unique opportunity to investigate the way a user can be so apathetic towards the technology at one moment, and then switch to being very passionate about acquiring one with a 'must have' attitude. As the study unfolded, this participant "fashioned" a DIY sock to keep his new device from being scratched, instead of buying one, because "they [commercially available cases] are too expensive". However, he did spend more money in buying more accessories to allow him to connect his new device into his car, to make it part of his daily journey. This behaviour was akin to building a long-term nest towards a long-term relationship with this device. He was falling in love. However, a strong sense of independence was shown by Andre (P-02), which was first exhibited in his rejection of the iPod brand as a fashion

Table 5.1 Summary of participant data. Numbers 1–4 are males, and 5–8 are females

No.	Name	Existing MP3 player	Prior usage-rate	New MP3 Player
P-01	Casper	None	N/A	iPod Touch
P-02	Andre	Creative Zen	Daily	Creative Vision
P-03	Marco	iPod shuffle	Daily	iPod Touch
P-04	Zed	Sony Ericson phone + iPod	Not much	iPod Touch
P-05	Jackie	iPod mini	Not often	iPod Nano
P-06	Lucy	Creative (small)	2–3 per week	iPod Mini
P-07	Betty	iPod mini + Sony NW-A2000	Daily	iPod Classic
P-08	Ellie	Creative Zen Micro	Rarely	iPod Nano

item, but more interestingly he saw himself as usually the one to "back the under-dog". He also gave another example of backing the underdog in other aspect of life (e.g. football team), and also said that he would usually not buy the "popular brand of car", but buy the lesser-known ones.

Marco (P-03) showed the type of behaviour where users will 'stalk' the market for the *right* version of the *right* product, with the *right* specifications. Having said that he was just about to buy the iPod Touch, he eventually waited seven months, for the next release. He did this, whilst monitoring the 'rumour' web sites that dis-cussed what the manufacturer might be doing. What was interesting is that this participant had a love of the product itself, but a deep dislike of the supplier's 'dictatorial and unfair way' that it treated its customers. Interestingly, the partici-pant that exhibited a self-constructing discourse the most, was Zed (P-04). He was careful in what he said during the interview, and was conscious of the impression he gave about himself, even though he was not known to the researcher at all, and was a complete stranger. To him, the MP3 player said volumes about the person using or owning it, and he wanted to control that. A striking aspect of Jackie's (P-05) experience was her very precise planning of exactly how, when and where she was going to buy her choice of MP3 player. This participant knew a lot about hand-held devices because she worked at a mobile phone shop, and she used this knowledge in order to understand the specifications (dimensions, weight etc.) as they were depicted on web sites. She had decided on the colour she wanted, and once in the shop, she bought the colour she planned. However, she then came back to swap it for a different colour. This was particularly interesting because, several times, this participant went out of her way to explain how colour is not an impor-tant aspect for her.

Lucy was a music graduate (P-06), and saw MP3 players as a time 'gap-filler', and was very uninterested in the technology itself. She was more interested in what it could do for her. She even found uploading new music to the device such a daunting task that she had never uploaded any more onto the device since the time she got it. So, what was originally uploaded is all she ever had, and she was happy with that. Her reporting that she was content with what she had, may have had an element of hiding any cognitive dissonance. In contrast, Betty is a drum-mer in a band (P-07), and saw that music is "what I'm about". She had decided against buying another iPod because of having a bad experience on the previous one, and then eventually did get an iPod as a birthday present. Betty's experience is described in more detail in the next case-study. Finally, Ellie (P-08) was particu-larly interesting because she spoke extensively about how she thought that iPods were a fashion gimmick and that she would never buy one. She bought an iPod Nano. Her justification was that it was a much reduced price, and therefore good value. She initially disliked iTunes (the iPod software), and eventually said that she was getting used it, and will probably like it.

The relative timeline of interviews for all the participants is shown in Fig. 5.2, where a total of 26 interviews were conducted, and recorded for audio, with 277 min total interview time. The average length of an interview was about eight minutes, although some interviews were almost 30 min.

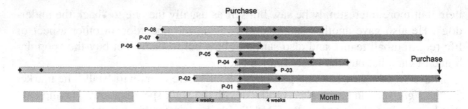

Fig. 5.2 Timing of interviews for all the participants (timescale is non-linear). Each *black-diamond* represents one interview. *Tan bars* are pre-purchase (or acquisition) phase, while *green bars* are post-purchase phase

5.4.2 Analysis

The results were analysed using the Content Analysis method described above. This section first describes the main emergent themes, and they are then listed in the context of the consumption phases (ABCD). Each phase is organised according to main themes found in the data. Almost all participants exhibited examples of all the following themes.

The first theme was **Convenience**, which is related to seemingly pragmatic aspects of the device. However, it would be naïve to consider such aspects as Compatibility or Size as innately 'pragmatic'. They are considered 'pragmatic' in the context of what a person is exposed in the wider culture, and are therefore essentially socially constructed. For this reason, 'pragmatic' is not used as a label in this context, because of the 'objective' connotation of the word. The theme of Convenience has the following sub-themes: *Size, Weight, Format, Compatibility, Dexterity, Ease of use, Learning, Battery, Capacity*. Next was the **Value** theme, which is related to other themes in the sense that value is the cost/benefit equation with any of the other themes, e.g. convenience, aesthetics or brand. For example, a participant may perceive a positive value for a device that offers high quality for the price they are paying, or they may perceive good value in getting a 'good brand' for a low price. The sub-themes of value are: *Cost* (monetary and otherwise), *Functions*, *Quality* of construction and performance, *Warranty*, and *Insurance* against obsolescence ("nice to know"). Therefore, their expectations and anticipations of such value are important. The **Relationship** theme is divided into three sub-themes: Relationship with *others* (friends, family, acquaintances), *Supplier and manufacturer* relationships, and Person-*object* relationships.

The theme was **Brand**, which is a complex construct in its own right, and in this study, participants regularly mentioned brand, and the 'myth' of the brand, in different ways. They used brand in relation to the other themes, and therefore, this theme can be seen as inseparable to the other themes. However, because brand itself was also used as a 'sign' in its own right, a promise and as a shortcut or pointer to the other themes (e.g. Trust, Reliability, Convenience and Compatibility), it warrants being treated separately. Brand is also a means of construction of the Self and a

Narrative. The sense of **Self** was also a theme that was ever present, and was linked to Aesthetics and Brand in many ways, but not always. Some participants saw the link with their identity and the functional aspect of MP3 players, i.e. to play music. Participants also indicated how the choice of devices was a means of *distinction* from other social groups, as part of the construction of themselves in an on-going narrative. They also showed aspects of *independence* and *dependence*, as well as being aware that they might be being left out, or being 'left behind', and therefore the need to 'keep up to date'. Finally, **Aesthetics** was also an emergent theme (linked to Self and Brand). However, the sub-themes are split into two basic types: *Formal* and *Expressive*. Formal aesthetics are those that are the subject of study in the field of 'New Experimental Aesthetics' (Berlyne 1974), such as complexity & novelty. Whereas Expressive aesthetics are those that are mostly the result of social constructs. Both sub-themes include visual, auditory and haptic stimuli.

5.4.3 Phases of Consumption

In this section, interview data are presented within the framework of the simplified consumption phases (ABCD). Quotations are referenced by the interview sequence number, e.g. "P-07b", the 'b' signifies the second interview, or group of questions in the interview schedule. Quotes will only be used once, although they may fit into more than one theme.

5.4.3.1 Approach

The Approach phase involves the user's attitudes to the technology item that is about to be acquired, and includes why they think they need or want it. Importantly, this stage encompasses the criteria for choice, as well as the sources of influence for the choices being considered.

Convenience: When asked about why he needed an MP3 player, participant P-02 said that he didn't need one per se, it was a matter of convenience to have his music collection at his disposal when on the move. He saw this as a luxury. Also, for participant P-08, she said that having an MP3 player contrasted with a CD player, in the sense it was less bulky and she did not have to carry CD's with her. In this way, an MP3 player is smaller, lighter and more compact. Also, when asked about the criteria for getting the next MP3 player, participants also cited convenience as part of the issues they paid attention to. Participant P-02 said that physical compactness as well as capacity (the amount of music a device can hold) were important: "fit in my hand, in my pocket, battery life, storage" (P-02a), while P-07 connected the two aspects of size and convenience: "Not to be too like bulky, so I can put it in my pocket. My Sony is too big" (P-07a). Ease-of-use was also seen as a particularly important criterion that is a matter of convenience. Participants seemed to be trying to avoid learning a new device, so remaining with the same brand is perceived to be a way of avoiding such effort.

Value: The notion of value also came up during the approach phase, where participants were actively looking at specific devices to buy. Therefore, comparing what they can buy in terms of functionality and quality for a particular amount of money. Other participants illustrated the notion of 'nice to know' as a way of adding to the value of a technological artifact. In this example, it is 'nice to know' that you may have the 'option' to do something: "it is nice to know it is there…[What does that mean?]… nice to have the variety in life, I can probably download episodes of a series, you wouldn't put a DVD collection on there, put a favourite Simpsons episode, it would be nice to pop that on, you don't have to go through it" (P-02d). In this example, the participant liked the idea that they 'could' if they wanted to, so it is a form of 'future proofing' against the possible desire or need. Therefore the value equation may be perceived to be related to the in the accumulation of options. In other words, the more technical options, features and specifications, the better value.

Relationship: The relationship with the supplier or brand was also apparent during the approach phase. In one example, the participant had originally planned to buy a particular model made by the Apple brand, but had put off the purchase due to rumours on the Internet regarding upgrades being available soon. According to his experience, this supplier had "done it before", and this made him suspicious that they would do it again: "Annoyed with Apple, not surprised. They have done it before. Staff are helpful when the product is new, but outside warranty, they don't care. Not fair. They charge MP3 users for updates, but not iPhone users. All users on the net are annoyed too" (P-03a). This shows a love/hate relationship with the supplier, where the users want the products and image of the product, yet they dislike the behaviour of the supplier. They seem to be able to separate the two, and can see a way of keeping the 'cool' part of the brand, and shunning the 'annoying' part of the brand.

Self: When asked about the reasons for feeling the need for an MP3 player, some participants connected this need to the way they defined or constructed themselves. The following two examples are quite strong. In the first, the participant sees himself as a DJ, and therefore music as an essential part of that role: "I DJ, so music all the time" (P-04a). The second example is even more telling where the participant clearly states "it's what I'm about", and also explains that it is related to her pastimes too: "cos I personally, I really like music, it's what I'm about, the music I play, I play drums, I'm in a band, I don't know, music is my favourite really" (P-07a). The next example of the theme of 'self' relates to how some participants use technology to distinguish themselves from particular groups of people. For example, P-02 emphasised the fact that he did not consider buying an Apple brand because of the meanings that he attributes to it, and the people that use and follow it. So, a criterion for the choice of a device is that it is 'not' related to that brand, as a way of defining himself. He goes on to give an example of the behaviour of the group of people that he does not associate with: "no, no didn't even consider it, I don't like them, cos everybody says, people don't say 'what MP3 player do you have?' they say 'what iPod do you have?' [I say] 'I don't have an iPod, I have an *MP3 player*'….It is the same with everything, it is the whole brandness, whenever a product gets dominated by a brand, I tend to stay away from it, I much prefer the underdog" (P-02d).

Brand: The issue of brand was also present during the approach phase, and in this example, it can be seen in the form of strong advocacy by friend: "I have a friend at Apple, he's a fanatic, he's like 'buy Apple buy Apple'. He has everything Apple, TV etc." (P-04a). The result of this recommendation was that the participant was a 'convert' and then became an advocate himself, by helping another friend obtain a product by the same brand: "She was 'I want an iPod'. Brand awareness. 'all my friends have iPods, I don't have one'. So, I bought her one." (P-04a).

Aesthetics: The formal aesthetic aspects of the device, e.g. complexity and simplicity appear to be relevant in the approach phase: "also the look of it as well, iPods look simple, they just look simple to use" (P-05a). However, it is important to note the such descriptors such as 'simple' are relative to what a user may be exposed to generally, and may also be the result of social representations that are in turn influenced by media exposure. With regards to colour, as a formal aesthetics property, an interesting reference to colour and 'self' was given by P-04, where he had the perception that all his 'stuff' is black, but then realised that maybe that is how he wanted it to be, rather than what reality was: "Probably get a black one again. I like all my stuff black. Actually, just my car. I like my car black. Nothing brighter (too girlie). Maybe go for something outrageous" (P-04a). So, for the above participant, colour is gendered, and black was a 'masculine' colour.

5.4.3.2 Buying (Acquisition)

The Buying (or Acquisition) phase is the point where the user actually is in possession of the technological artifact, or just before. This is the point where the choice has been operationalised, and is not a hypothetical choice. This phase is also the point where the users may reflect on their choice and the purchasing experience.

Convenience: When asked about the factors that influence the eventual purchase of the MP3 player, convenience was highlighted by P-02, as something he was thinking about when searching, and he saw the brand as a signpost to convenience, for example: "keep the brand for convenience of transfer" (P-02b). Conversely P-08 conveyed her annoyance at being inconvenienced by the time taken when being forced to convert her music files to a new format required by her new device: "Annoyed about converting to iPod format... took ages to convert to iPod format. Really annoying" (P-08b).

Value: When asked if other models of MP3 players were contenders for purchase, P-07 cited her perception of the capacity/price equation for value: "yeah, I looked at a few, but ... it had loads of memory, the one that I got, for some of them, they're a little bit cheaper, but its worth paying like an extra 30 pounds or something to get for like what you're getting, you get loads more" (P-07b).

Relationship: When referring to the search activity, P-07 mentioned the involvement of reviews from other users in her decision: "I searched on loads of web sites, but in the end I think my dad got it from Amazon...there are some reviews that I looked at." Also, one of the participants' decision was entirely based on her friend's choice, as her friend gave her a previously used device as a gift: "Instead of buying an MP3 player my friend gave me their old one [an iPod Mini]" (P-06bc).

Self: During the buying phase, 'self' was an apparent theme in different ways. One way was relevant to the way the participant saw and understood themselves. In the following example, P-01 understands himself as a person that has difficulty with technological devices. He also relates his tendency of not reading the user manual, as an aspect of masculinity as well as being related to his dyslexic condition: "I am someone who has difficulty understanding these things (DVD, TV etc.), without looking at the manual for months. I am dyslexic, and I am sure there is this masculine 'I am sure I can work it out on my own if I persevere'" (P-01ab).

When considering factors and criteria for which device to buy, one participant saw themselves as a 'pragmatic' and 'functional' buyer, which he implied to be a positive value in a person. Participant P-02 gave such an example when discussing his criteria. He said that the value equation for him was purely price versus function.

Brand: When describing his purchasing experience, P-01 commented on the presentation of the device and how the way it was packaged was "very iPod". He then contrasted the brand image of the device he bought with other suppliers, which further strengthened his conviction of how he saw the brand he had bought: "Stickers, makes you smile, little screen wiper cloth… very iPod [smile]… slim-line…PC industry boxing is usually ten times the size of the item. Re-emphasize positive impression of efficiency of iPod" (P-01ab). Therefore, in this example, this participant describes how the brand is a signpost for 'efficiency'.

Aesthetics: The question of the purchasing experience as a whole was raised for P-05. Her response focused on what seems to be a self-construction, as well as colour preference due to individual differences: "it was a bit rushed…. I was being indecisive with my colours… then I picked one, then I bought it, then I changed my mind and completely different colour one… didn't think it would be the same [colour] as real life, which I don't think it was, it was a lot more metallic in real life…. I knew it was going to look different, that's why I wanted to see them… obviously on a computer screen, you can't see the metallicness of it, I wanted to double-check in real life that it was the colour that I wanted… in terms of colour, I'm not fussed, I would have been happy with the pink one, and I would have been happy with the green one, which is the other colour I would have gone for, I'm not really fussed about the colour… it was a hot pink, and an Appley shiny green." (P-05b). This participant talked a lot about the colour of the device, yet made a point of saying the she was "not fussed" about colour. This shows an interesting contradiction of what the participant is apparently paying a great deal of attention to, and what she says. She therefore constructs herself as someone that does not see colour as important, yet her behaviour shows she does.

5.4.3.3 Consummation (Use)

The Consummation phase is where actual use has taken place, and the anticipations have been fulfilled and/or disappointments have ensued. This is the phase where recommendations are in the form of informed judgements.

Convenience: Compatibility becomes much more of an immediate issue once actual consumption and use takes place, as P-01 points out: "Music and video, format, conversion (takes a lot of time), compatibility is an issue" (P-01c). Such issues lead to convenience or inconvenience, as the case may be. The convenience of the device is highlighted also by P-03. This time it is about how the technology is working to create more leisure time: "you can do so much with it, and it's really cut down the amount of time I use my PC, because I check my emails in the morning before my lectures, and I check my emails while I am in my lectures, I use my laptop now once a day, rather than 3 or 4 times a day, it gives you more free time really" (P-03c).

Value: The sense of value was also apparent during use. One participant discussed how he evaluates the value in having a small screen on an MP3 player that enables watching a film. He considers the value as more of a luxury or toy. However, he also acknowledges that to be a form 'insurance', in case he finds himself in a situation that he may use it, i.e. 'nice to know'. In some sense, attributing value to convenience.

Relationship: During the consummation phase, there were examples of three types of relationships being manifest. First there was the relationship with friends and family, providing word or mouth recommendations or otherwise. An example of this was given by P-01, where he took the opportunity to relay a story that would become part of the overall narrative of his experience with the device: "Have recommended it to family and a couple of friends… nice to see the envious looks on their face…. I'll tell you a funny story… inadvertently showed it off to head of development of Sony" (P-01c). The second type of relationship that was illustrated during this phase was that of a user-object type, which also had aspects of the relationship between the user and manufacturer. Some relationships were about collecting 'satellite' objects and accessories for the main object itself. However, another type of object relationship was more about the object 'mediating' other relationships, and becoming a token for person-to-person relationship, and so the value in the MP3 players is not the device itself, rather the personal data and photographs of people in meaningful relationships: "I would be sad if I lost it… photos of loved ones on there" (P-02c). The third type of relationship that was seen during this phase is that concerning the supplier of the device. Some participants commented on the purchasing or consuming experience in relation to the supplier, where for example a device had been faulty, and they relayed the details of how the supplier or seller behaved.

Self: The theme of 'self' was also visible during the consummation phase and in the following example, P-04 found it important to avoid embarrassment by not having a 'basic' device. He took this further by seeing it important to have and show himself as having 'iPod Touch', which is a way of distinguishing himself amongst his peers: "Not embarrassed to show friends you had it. If I got a basic one, I wouldn't have raved about it. But now that I have the iPod Touch…I'm like 'I got the iPod Touch, you haven't'" (P-04bc).

Brand: Brand was also a topic that participants discussed during the consummation phase, and this was in the form of what the brand was a pointer to, or a signifier for. For example, when asked about why he bought the same brand, one participant anticipated using the same brand because it was a pointer to convenience: "cos they are the only MP3 players I have ever owned... menu, actual text of the menu and the way you scroll through has been exactly the same... I had my music on it within 10 min...I knew where everything would be straight away, ... didn't have to install any software, just plugged it in... it was done straight away, I just didn't want to go through the rigmarole of having to change it" (P-02d). Therefore, the convenience that the brand offered equated to a reduction of the potential cost, i.e. effort. Other brands were anticipated to be a 'rigmarole', and therefore being a pointer to 'stress'.

Aesthetics: Aesthetics still played a role during the consummation stage, albeit in a subdued manner. When asked about how he was getting on with the new device, P-01 said that the novelty aspect of the device was now diminishing: "I feel the novelty is wearing off now" (P-01c). This reduction in novelty was also echoed by P-08, who also expressed a realisation that maybe she had spent too much on something that no longer seemed so valuable, even though she still liked it. However, it was not just the novelty and formal aspects of aesthetics that were discussed. Some participants, noted a change in the way they valued the expressive and creative aesthetics: "I would prefer the colour to be broken-up. It is all black" (P-05c).

5.4.3.4 Dissolution and Divestment

This phase of the consumption cycle relates to the point where users are divesting, somehow, of their 'previous device' (that was owned or used prior to the start of the interviews), or the device that most closely performed the function of the next one. It is also the phase where they are ending or changing the relationship with the previous device in favour of a newer relationship.

Convenience: Convenience was an important factor during the dissolution phase. For example, when asked about the previously owned device, P-05 was inconvenienced when the battery did not work well: "the battery keeps dying, it says its dying even though it's fully charged and I've just charged it, 20 min later it's dead and cold, so I can't really take it out or play it at home" (P-05a). Also, ease-of-use was a factor, for example, P-05 and P-07 said that they liked the ease-of-use aspect of their previous devices: "the iPod is really easy to use and it's simple to transfer data." (P-07a), and, "quite easy, it's got a USB cable, it plugs into the bottom of it, then it just recognises it, opens up iTunes" (P-05a). In the above example, P-05 also mentions aspect of connectivity that are related to the format or standard of connection, in this case the USB connector makes it easy to use, and the fact that the device is 'just recognised' is an indication of how convenient the operation is.

Value: P-05 sensed a lack of value in what she owned, in comparison to other model, even when she did not have any knowledge of other models. She suggested that her current device was out-dated and obsolete, and knew that current models gave better value: "it's kind of quite old now, the screen is not colour, it's just the normal, it doesn't play videos, which a lot of them do now, and it doesn't hold pictures, which a lot of them do, I think it's quite small, but its quite big in comparison to the newer ones" (P-05). When the participants were asked about how they intended to divest their old device, the perceived value of previous devices was also illustrated, and the participants offered a range of responses. Some saw it as worthless, some thought to store it in the loft and some would gift it. "I don't know, just put it in the loft [laugh]" (P-05a), "there is nothing wrong with it, so probably give it to my young cousin" (P-06a).

Relationship: As far as the different types of relationships in the dissolution phase, participants referenced examples where they have been influenced by their friends. However, participants also showed that a relationship with a friend could be mediated through the device. In this case, the technological aspect or function is not central: "you can personalise it, I got it engraved for my girlfriend, none of the other MP3 players, you can do that with" (P-04a). In the above example, the perception that the device can be personalised, and therefore enhance the participant's relationship with his friend, enrich his experience of the device, and he made his choice partly based on this option. Equally, some participants had no attachment to the device.

Self: There were examples of participants recalling their previous purchases as part of a narrative they were engaged in authoring, as well as actively constructing themselves. For example, P-04 explained the circumstances of his previous purchase: "got it so I could say I had biggest Nano iPod. No research, just knew iPods were good" (P-04a). Another aspect of 'the self' is where participants engaged in defining themselves, in the context of unfolding events. For example, P-06 explained the way she used her previous (outgoing) device: "I like it cos it's small, I thought it would be easy to use, it is easy to use... I don't know, it is a USB, you download it, and I'm not very good at what I've got on there, I tend to just keep what I've got on there" (P-06a). In the above example, there were many references to "I", and P-06 explains her usage in terms of what she is able or not able to do. So, she is content with its performance and capacity, even though she finds it difficult to use. Therefore, self-blame and self-deprecation is one way that this participant is making sense of her experience with this device. In this way, the narrative of the experience with this device is perhaps helping shape this participant's construction of herself.

Brand: An interesting reference to brand during the dissolution phase was given by P-07. The participant illustrates the use of brand as concurrently a signpost to quality "one of the best", as well as a signpost to negative experiences "iPods have broke". She goes on to describe what the brand also points to: "good software" and "ease of use", as well as the "cool...stylish" perceptions, which may have links to what the participant hopes to weave into how she constructs her sense of self. Ultimately P-07 declares the decision to opt "for a different brand". So, her choice is still using the brand as a signpost, rather than make an active choice based on any other criteria, such as function, capacity etc. This example is discussed in detail in case-study 4.

Aesthetics: An important role was also played by aesthetics, as seen in other themes in this phase. However, by way of specific responses, the following examples show references to the aesthetic value given to previous devices. When asked what she thought of her previous model, P-08 said that: "it's a brick, fine before, but now… black and white was OK before, but not now…its rubbish" (P-08a). As she says, it represented good aesthetic value (colour and form) at some point in the past, and perhaps had a novel aspect to it, but it no longer did.

5.5 Betty's iPod (Case-Study 4)

Betty (P-07 in case-study 3) had an overall negative experience during the time of the case-study. There is no implication intended that negative or positive experiences are more or less important than each other. An important aspect of relaying Betty's story is to show a connected 'individual history' that provides the background to the experiences as they unfold, rather than being isolated or generic events. As will be seen, this case-study is discussed initially in an approximate chronological order, though it is also used to illustrate brand resilience, as well as the way that identity is associated with many aspects of the experience.

Throughout the study, Betty's sense of 'self' seemed to have been an important underlying factor, and was perhaps partly driving the whole experience and narrative, to the extent that when asked about why she felt that she needed an MP3 player, her response was: "I really like music, *it's what I'm about*…I play drums, I'm in a band". Betty had an iPod, and Sony MP3 player, and had bad experiences with the current iPod, and did not like the Sony device (she thought it the Sony model was not easy to use). She approached the purchase in two minds, and this manifested itself in a split opinion: "decided to go for a different brand [not Apple]… but I still think that iPod is probably best… cool… quite stylish". Cool and stylish is perhaps how Betty sees herself too. However, as her experience started to unfold, she perceived the iPod to be good value, with its 'high capacity', 'low price', and extra functionality that allowed video playback as something "Nice to know you could do that". Importantly, 'ease of use' was high on the list of factors that were important for Betty. In fact, within about four minutes into the same interview, Betty, had changed her mind, and decided to buy an iPod: "I think I will get an iPod, but I'm not sure, which one to get. The new touch screen… might invest in that one… I think it is worth investing in like a better one… it is better to invest in a better one than compromise, and save a bit of money". This decision seemed to have been mixed up with the sense of value of the purchase, where 'investment' is a factor. Betty did get an iPod as a birthday gift from her father, who purchased it from an online supplier, Amazon, which is a supplier that she "could trust". She chose a model, and paid extra where she was convinced that she would get increased value: "an extra £30 or something to get … loads more."

However, the anticipations during the approach and buying phases, were eventually unfulfilled during the later phase of consummation. These positive anticipations turned into frustrations, disenchantment and eventually annoyance, and perhaps even anger. Betty summarised her experience as "I was getting on well, but it broke about a week ago, which I am not happy about at all... at first the pictures stopped showing, so I resetted it... but now keeps on resetting itself, its just sort of stuck in a constant like loop of resetting itself, so I just can't do anything with it, I'll just have to send it back... I used it for about a week, six days or something, like it was good for those six days". Betty then contrasted the negative outcome and explained the positive aspects of her experience, related to the convenience derived from speed. She then began exploring the overall evaluative and emotional elements of her experience "but now its broken, only had it for a few weeks and it broke, so, I'm really disappointed with it." Betty explained that she "thought that you could take it back to the shop... but apparently not." These feelings later took on a different quality, where 'worry' and surprise ("surprised by the fact that it broke"), become evident. She was now exhibiting constant flitting between negative and positive aspects of the device, as she was trying to make sense of her experience. Winter et al. (2008) quote Kelly's term of "slot rattling" to describe these types of bipolar swings in a relationship (2008, p. 90).

Ultimately though, when Betty was asked if she would recommend the device she bought, her answer was interesting: "yeah, well, yeah probably, I probably would, even, yeah I probably would...as I say, it's cool, easy to use, *it's a good MP3 player*, it is good, it is good." This experience later unfolded into further negativity where the supplier and the manufacturer where not taking responsibility for fixing the device and ended up getting a refund. When asked if she was going to buy an iPod again, Betty replied: "Yes I think I will, but I have got some doubt though... cos my last iPod went wrong, and that's kind of confirmed it". And when asked again if she would get another 'Apple', Betty answered "Yes, the thing is that I do want to get an iPod, because they are the best, and its going to be easiest to use...oh [frustrated] I don't know...I do want one, cos obviously it's the easiest to use, and I think it is the iPod [interrupts self] the MP3 player for me, but at the same time, I don't know, if it not going to be reliable... and the service is bad as well, cos no one was taking responsibility." Betty then makes a clear statement on what could be an extremely important aspect of what she meant by 'easy': "I do want it because its easy to use, iTunes is easy and also if I use iTunes, my friend's got a program, cos normally if you plug an iPod into a friends computer, you can't get music off it, my friend's got a program where you can ... So when one of my friends from home, so when he comes up he can, he finds out music before I do, which means he can bring his iPod, and just connect it into my computer and I can get all the music, so it is going to be really easy to use, And it looks good." The convenience of being able to 'just connect' to her friend's computer, and share music is obviously something important to her, and she perceives it to be difficult, or not 'easy' if she were to get a different brand. She does not want to lose this facility and connection with her friend. And in this example, another brand 'means', or is a signpost to, the loss of this aspect of her relationship with her friend. Therefore, once again, Betty questions the value equation and her judgement, where she may be placing 'reliability' too low on the priority order: "in theory its perfect... I don't want to buy it and then keep on breaking... I am thinking maybe it is better to buy one that is more reliable, but isn't as easy to use."

When asked about her knowledge of easy to use devices, Betty acknowledges that all she knows about other models is based on her knowledge of her other device, the Sony branded model, which was already established as an awkward device. Betty then begins to formulate other theories and starts to explore possibilities that may make more sense of her experience. However, as a summary evaluation, she summarises her experience as one with many contradictions and disappointments, to arrive at a point of being annoyed: "I thought it was going to be simple ... I didn't realise so many things are going to go wrong, I thought it was going to be simple, I should be having my iPod now, it's quite annoying."

Eventually, however, when asked what she would do next, Betty confirmed that she will try to somehow address the reliability issue by trying to hold one reputable supplier responsible, but ultimately, she will be buying another iPod: "I probably will buy an iPod I think ... what I might do is probably buy it from the Apple-store ... at least I've got the peace of mind that if anything goes wrong, I can just go there and they should fix it." Therefore, according to Betty, she can remove the 'inconvenience' element of her experience by simplifying her relationship with the supplier and making sure the supplier is trustworthy.

Interestingly, Betty did not consider that a Sony device could become easier to use, she insisted on seeing if iPod could become more reliable. This may be an indicator that really she wanted Apple, at whatever cost. The iPod may have given her a totem of her identity ("it is what I'm about"), or it may have given her access to the fresh music supply from her friend. Or even the ability to sustain the particular relationship with her friend. Therefore, if she got a Sony branded device, she may jeopardise that relationship. Therefore, it may be that Betty was giving the reason of 'ease of use' as a way of ensuring that she was seen to be a 'rational' consumer.

5.6 Summary

This chapter was chiefly concerned with the longer term dynamics of UX, as well as exploring UX from a more holistic point of view, with the aim of revealing the way users made sense of their experience. Consumption was argued to be a useful analogue to experience, and the case-studies were chosen to explore people's experience of consuming media devices. The case-studies examined here re-iterated some of the findings in the first two case-studies, and showed additional super-constructs that contribute a holistic experience with technology: *Convenience, Value, Relationship, Self, Brand* and *Aesthetics*. The findings have also shown how experience is based on an intricate network of implications and other constructions, where such a network has a strong influence on overall evaluations, affect and decision processes. These data will be used in the next chapter in order to suggest how a general theory of UX may be used in order to understand people's experience in terms of ICE: *interaction, construction,* and *evaluation.*

References

Andrews, L., Drennan, J., & Bennett, R. (2005). *Emotions In The Experiential Consumption Of Mobile Phones*. Paper presented at the ANZMAC 2005 Conference: Electronic Marketing.

Arnould, E., Price, L., & Zinkhan, G. (2004). *Consumers* (Vol. 2nd). New Jersey: McGraw-Hill Publishing Company.

Barnes, N. G. (1986). The consumer decision process for professional services marketing: A new perspective. *Journal of Professional Services Marketing, 2*(1/2), 39–45.

Berlyne, D. E. (1974). *Studies in the new experimental aesthetics: Steps toward an objective psychology of aesthetic appreciation*. Washington D.C.: Halsted Press.

Blackwell, R. D., Miniard, P. W., & Engel, J. F. (2006). *Consumer Behaviour: International Student Edition* (Vol. 10). Mason OH, USA: Thompson.

Bourdieu, P. (1984). *Distinction: A social critique of the judgement of taste*. London: Routledge.

Carù, A., & Cova, B. (2007). Consuming experience: An introduction. In A. Carù & B. Cova (Eds.), *Consuming experience* (pp. 3–16). Abingdon: Routledge.

Christopher, K. H., Zhang, J., Yu, F., & Xi, Y. (2003). Lay rationalism and inconsistency between predicted experience and decision. *Journal of Behavioral Decision Making, 16*(4), 257–277.

Engel, J. F., Kollat, D., & Blackwell, R. D. (1968). *Consumer behaviour*. New York: Holt, Rinehart and Winston.

Fajer, M. T., & Schouten, J. W. (1995). Breakdown and dissolution of person-brand relationships. *Advances in Consumer Research, 22*, 663–667.

Foxall, G. R., & Goldsmith, R. E. (1994). *Consumer psychology for marketing*. London: Routledge.

Hansen, T. (2005). Perspectives on consumer decision making: An integrated approach. *Journal of Consumer Behaviour, 4*(6), 420–437.

Hassenzahl, M. (2004). The interplay of beauty, goodness, and usability in interactive products. *Human-Computer Interactions, 19*, 319–349.

Hoeffler, S. (2003). Measuring preferences for really new products. *Journal of Marketing Research, 40*(4), 406–420.

Holbrook, M. B., & Hirschman, E. C. (1982). The experiential aspects of consumption: consumer fantasies, feelings, and fun. *The Journal of Consumer Research, 9*(2), 132–140.

Holt, D. B. (1995). How consumers consume: a typology of consumption practices. *Journal of Consumer Research, 22*, 1–16.

Howard, J. A., & Sheth, J. N. (1969). *The theory of buyer behaviour*. New York: Wiley.

Karapanos, E., Zimmerman, J., Forlizzi, J., & Martens, J.-B. (2009). *User Experience over time: An initial framework*. Paper presented at the The CHI Conference on Computer-Human Interaction—SIG, Boston, USA.

Kelly, G. A. (1955). *The Psychology of Personal Constructs, Volume One: Theory and Personality* (1991 ed. Vol. 1). London: Routledge.

Kelly, G. A. (2003). A brief introduction to personal construct theory. In F. Fransella (Ed.), *International handbook of personal construct psychology*. Chichester: Wiley.

Kumar, V. (2013). *101 design methods: A structured approach for driving innovation in your organisation*. Hoboken: Wiley.

Lindgaard, G., Fernandes, G., Dudek, C., & Brown, J. (2006). Attention web designers: You have 50 milliseconds to make a good first impression! *Behaviour and Information Technology, 25*(2), 115–126.

Maslow, A. H. (1987). *Motivation and Personality* (Vol. 3). New York: HarperCollins.

McCarthy, J., & Wright, P. C. (2004). *Technology as experience*. Cambridge.: MIT Press.

Mehrabian, A., & Russell, J. A. (1974). *An approach to environmental psychology*. Cambridge: MIT Press.

Minge, M. (2008). *Dynamics of user experience*. Paper presented at the Research Goals and Strategies for Studying User Experience and Emotion—NordiCHI2008, Lund, Sweden.

Mowen, J. C. (1988). Beyond consumer decision making. *The Journal of Consumer Marketing, 5*(1), 15–25.

Nicosia, F. M. (1966). *Consumer decision processes: Marketing and advertising implications.* New Jersey: Prentice Hall.

Nielson, J. (1994). *Usability engineering (interactive technologies).* San Francisco: Morgan Kaufmann.

Norman, D. A. (2009). Systems thinking: A product is more than the product. *Interactions, 16*(5), 52–54.

Pham, M. T. (1995). Anticipations and consumer decision making. *Advances in Consumer Research, 22,* 275–276.

Pinch, T., & Bijker, W. (1987). The social construction of facts and artifacts: or how the sociology of technology might benefit each other. In W. Bijker, J. Huges, & T. Pinch (Eds.), *The social construction of technical systems.* Cambridge: MIT Press.

Rogers, E. M. (2003). *Diffusion of Innovations* (Vol. 5th). New York: Simon and Schuster International.

Solomon, M., Bamossy, G., Askegaard, S., Hogg, M. K. (2006). *Consumer behaviour: A European perspective* (Vol. 3rd). Harlow: Prentice Hall.

Swallow, D., Blyth, M. A., & Wright, P. C. (2005). *Grounding experience: Relating theory and method to evaluate the user experience of smartphones. Paper presented at the Proceedings of the 2005 annual conference on European association of cognitive ergonomics.*

Thüring, M., & Mahlke, S. (2007). Usability, aesthetics, and emotions in human-technology-interaction. *International Journal of Psychology, 42,* 253–264.

Tractinsky, N., Shoval-Katz, A., & Ikar, D. (2000). What is beautiful is usable. *Interacting with Computers, 13,* 127–145.

von Wilamowitz-Moellendorff, M., Hassenzahl, M., Platz, A. (2006). *Dynamics of User Experience: How the perceived quality of mobile phones changes over time. Paper presented at the User Experience: Towards a unified view—COST294-MAUSE.*

Vyas, D., van der Veer, G. C. (2006). *Rich evaluations of entertainment experience—bridging the interpretational gap. Paper presented at the 13th European conference on Cognitive ergonomics: trust and control in complex socio-technical systems, Zurich, Switzerland.*

Winter, D. A., Duncan, J., & Summerfield, E. (2008). Love hurts: Exploration of love validation and conflict. *Personal Construct Theory and Practice, 5,* 86–98.

Zajonc, R. B., & Markus, H. (1982). Affective and cognitive factors in preferences. *Journal of Consumer Research, 9*(2), 123–131.

Chapter 6
ICE: A Model of Experience with Technology

Abstract The ICE model is described in detail in the light of discussions in the earlier chapters and the main findings from the four case-studies. Constructs are discussed within the context of dynamics, anticipation, and the way in which constructs relate to each other, including the stability of constructs as a dimension relevant to UX dynamics. The super-constructs are also summarised at this point: *Novelty, Usability, Complexity, Aesthetics, Physicality, Value,* and *Convenience.* Interaction and evaluation, the other two aspects of ICE, are also discussed in detail. In addition, the concept of relationships is addressed from several different points of view: relationship as a way of defining self, the relationship users have with brand, how relationship is used as a proxy for other experiences, and the relationship users have with objects. Finally, the concept of *user experience networks* is proposed as fundamental to the way in which experiences relate to each other, and therefore influence how people experience technology. Implications of this emergent attribute are discussed.

Keywords Anticipation • Construction • Interaction • Evaluation • Relations hips • Self • ICE model • Human–computer interaction (HCI) • Mobile device usability • Personal Construct Theory (PCT) • Sense making • User experience (UX) • User experience dynamics

6.1 Processes of ICE

The overall concept of ICE was introduced in Sect. 2.2.4, and the data presented in the case-studies will be used here to address the first research question which is about the way users make meaning as they experience technology, as well as the second question regarding the nature of UX and its underlying constructs. This discussion will be undertaken by stepping through the primary processes of ICE: *interaction, construction,* and *evaluation.*

6.1.1 Construction

The variety of constructs shown by the sorting tasks have revealed that the participants really were focusing on different aspects of the MP3 players, and they were also giving meaning in a rich and varied way. The very act of sorting provided a window to the sense-making processes themselves, as the category labels provided further granularity to the structure of the meanings that were available in the repertoire of the users.

Aside from the main themes of constructs found in in the case-studies, there were many examples of idiosyncratic constructs (e.g. Holiday), showing a wide distribution of constructs, for example, for 'Kinds of Beauty', these constructs ranged from *symmetry*, *sleek* and *simple* to *trendy*, *striking* and *eye-catching*, as well as *technological*, *futuristic* and *classic*. Some constructs were re-iterated by several participants, while others were only referenced once, and this pattern approximately followed a power distribution. Such patterns occur naturally and they are given different names in different disciplines e.g. Zipf and Pareto distributions (Zipf 1949). They are also referred to as "The Long Tail" (Anderson 2004).

By considering the properties of the MP3 players in relation to one another, the participants in Study-1 were afforded the opportunity to reflect on the constructs that they applied towards understanding the devices. Whilst distinct objective parameters were frequently discussed such as 'rectangular' (portrait and landscape orientations), 'curved' and 'irregular' shapes, these linked to more subjective and evaluative understandings. However, these objective properties are not transparent to the researcher, and the MSA plots have served to elucidate the objective qualities of the object, where "objective qualities only serve the purpose of recognition" (Csikszentmihalyi and Rochberg-Halton 1981, p. 180). In this way, the participant may have sorted a non-visual attribute, but they were able to do so, by recognising the visual 'sign' of the non-physical attribute, and therefore articulating constructs by 'comparison'. Study-1 has also allowed access to the sense-making processes even to the extent of being able to track them in real-time. Real-time recordings of the sorting tasks were made, where the participants were actively constructing alternative 'realities' and interpreting them according to past experiences. There were also demonstrations of how preferences can change in an instant, based on some new and alternative construction, in line with Kelly's constructive alternativism. When the participants were sorting the photographs, they were reflecting on past experiences and also making pre-linguistic connections (such as colour or shape preference). They would sometimes deliberate on which pile (category) to place the cards, and other times, make an instant decision. There were also times where the instant decisions were reversed, without hesitation. There were several examples of how the methodology described in Study-1 has demonstrated the sense-making framework described by McCarthy and Wright (2004) as a useful approach and a way of categorising the way that individuals made sense of their world, e.g. the illustrations of reflection, interpretation and recounting of actual and anticipated experiences and events. This shows the strength of the sorting technique in being able to detect and illustrate the reconstruing process as it happens, and thereby allowing the researcher to probe and investigate these events in real-time. These construing and reconstruing episodes ultimately enriched and informed the data, both the qualitative and quantitative. It is therefore possible to suggest that this methodology (combination of MSP and MSA/SSA) and approach provides a window onto the theoretical, constructive and sense-making world of 'user the scientist'.

Of course these constructs, super-constructs, and their evaluations are not objective properties which can be scored on an absolute scale. For example, what is novel to one person, may not be novel to another. What they do show however, is that 'novelty' is something that people pay attention to, implicitly or explicitly, and this aspect plays an important role in their experience of technology. Although Study-2 measured the direction of rating changes, there is no importance implied to that direction in the general analysis of the data. Such directionality may be the domain of individual differences that dictate personal taste and personality traits.

However, on the whole, there were seven overarching themes, dimensions or super-constructs. Of these, *Novelty* and *Complexity* confirm the earlier positions derived in the *New Experimental Aesthetics* studies of the 1970s (e.g. Berlyne 1974), where the emphasis was on finding 'objective' constructs relating to visual stimuli. These aspects have also been shown to be present specifically within technological experiences (Huang 2003). However, Berlyne's early work was undertaken using isolated geometric patterns, rather than whole stimuli situated in an environment that is familiar to participants. The main criticism of these findings is that they may be too reductive, by isolating novelty to a matter of geometric patterns. Nonetheless, these lab-based stimuli of geometric patterns showed that people are sensitive to novelty in relation to preference, but did not test novelty in the real world. Finding novelty and complexity dimensions amongst the data from the studies in this research, not only shows that people are sensitive to novelty, but also shows in what way. In other words, people are sensitive to novelty and complexity when it comes to MP3 players, and these constructs refer to novelty or complexity in aspects other than the purely visual, e.g. function, operation, concept etc. In particular, Study-1 data showed a split in the grouping of the MP3 player preference between simple designs and non-simple designs. This was seen to be a similar split illustrated with research regarding preferences of architecture of buildings, where there was a distinction between modern and post-modern styles (Wilson 1996).

Study-3 showed further super-constructs to add to the initial five. *Value* was one of the new super-constructs which, aside from the cost/benefit equation discussed earlier, was also described by Richins (1994, p. 506) to be of different types (see Chap. 3), where Richins categorises value to be: *utilitarian, enjoyment, financial, self-identity, relationship*. There were several examples of the utilitarian and financial aspects of value. There were also examples of participants valuing aspects of technology that helped them create their self-identity, and enhance their relationship with others (Dittmar 2008). This sense of value can also be enhanced over time, also referred to as 'Patina', i.e. an artifact becomes more valuable the more it shows signs of use, e.g. aging and wear. An example of this was seen when participants reported a sense of their MP3 player becoming more personal when photographs and personal choice of music were uploaded to the device (Study-3). However, value can also be seen in the 'history' of an artifact before acquisition takes place. According to Marx (1978), *"articles of utility become commodities"* (1978, p. 321) and some of their value is in the labour-time of their production. In other words, the value is in the type and amount of work undertaken to create it.

Also, the super-construct of *Convenience* has been shown in the data across some of the studies in this book. This category includes aspects such as pragmatics, compatibility, as well as compactness (which is of course related to physicality). Although the decision making process is not of interest in this book, the data do show that aspects of convenience play a role in preference and decision making, which have sometimes led to directly influencing behavioural outcomes such as buying decisions.

A particularly interesting new finding was the unusual relationship between the above super-constructs and *Aesthetics* (Study-2). Participants were sensitive to the aesthetic aspects of the photographs, where the analysis showed aesthetics to be a separate super-construct that is closely related to usability and novelty. However, once physical interaction took place, aesthetics were then connected to physicality and complexity, to the extent that aesthetics became subsumed by other super-constructs to become more holistic. This 'move' gives a clue to construction being based initially on *indirect experiences* (inferences and anticipations), and then made through interaction as *direct experience*. The aesthetics move demonstrates the re-evaluation that took place post-interaction. As discussed earlier in Chap. 3, aesthetics was shown to be perceived 'remotely', i.e. just from the photograph, as well as through interaction.

A possible explanation for the above result is that the aesthetic aspects are initially dominated by visual perception and anticipations. However, as a result of interaction, the user is given the opportunity to reconstrue the visual stimulus, using additional senses e.g. haptic and sonic. As a result, the aesthetic aspects then become grounded in physical interaction in the Life-World, rather than a reflective or anticipatory interaction that resides in a cognitive realm. For these reasons, aesthetics become much more related to Physicality. Also, Novelty and Complexity become part of the device *in use* rather than in detached reflection. It is interesting to note that out of all the super-constructs, Aesthetics is the only one that changes its relation to the others, and behaves more like a 'binding agent', acting as a bridge between them all. In other words, once interaction takes place, there is an overall evaluative judgment that is common to all super-constructs, regardless of the particular judgment for one of them. This may be related to the idea of "what is beautiful is usable" (Tractinsky et al. 2000), where for example, the aesthetic constructs became more correlated to the usability constructs after interaction took place (Study-2). However, there were several examples of brand overshadowing negative aspects of usability and quality. For example, when participants came across usability problems during the interaction sessions of Study-2, they were happy to be more 'forgiving' when using a well-known brand, but not so when dealing with an unknown brand. Therefore, the assertion that "what is beautiful is usable" (Tractinsky et al. 2000), may be missing the essence of such an effect, which is the brand or 'narrative' that underlies the artifact. A strong demonstration of this resilience of brand was also shown in Study-4.

These findings begin to explain how some traditional concepts in aesthetics apply to the interaction with digital products. For example, Lang (1988) suggested three types of aesthetics: *sensory*, *formal* and *symbolic*, while Nohl (1988) separated aesthetics into *perceptual*, *symptomatic* and *symbolic*. Here, sensory (or perceptual) aesthetics are related to sound, colour, odour etc., which involve the arousal of the user's perceptual system. Formal aesthetics involve the shape, rhythm and complexities of the scene, whereas symptomatic aesthetics relate to what the shape is a symptom of. For example, a large bulky battery may be a 'symptom' of a high battery capacity, or a thin laptop may be a symptom of 'latest technology'. Symbolic aesthetics, however, signify aspects that are perhaps not directly related to the scene. In the case of technology, this could be culturally shared meanings associated with a brand, or colour. Lavie and Tractinsky (2004) also argued for similar distinctions of *Classical* and *Expressive* aesthetics.

6.1.2 Interaction

Undoubtedly, physical and virtual interaction can play major roles in the use of technology, though such definitions may be limiting, and miss other ways that people *interact* with technology. In Study-1, the participants were consistently referred to as 'users' in. This could raise the objection that the participants did not 'use' the devices, but only viewed life-sized photographs. However, for the reasons outlined above, it could be argued that a user, is not just a person who is physically interacting with the particular artifact, but one who is construing the artifact with 'use' in mind, and is therefore judging and evaluating it from the point of their past and future experience with similar products. Therefore, the photographs are not sterile images, but images that are laden with promise, action and implications in the 'real world'. For example, in Study-1 and the visual part of Study-2, there were examples of projections of 'fit' and 'non-fit' where the participants would construct a 'theory' of whether a particular item would match other scenarios and aspects of their life or whether it would be out of place and they just "could not see it." This theory building seems to be linked to the basis of preference towards the item in question. Participants also showed that they could quickly change their preference with an alternative construction, as soon as they had some new piece of information or a new feasible scenario being presented.

The semiotics field of research is full of work on how the world is replete with visual symbols (features, shapes, colours, brand etc.) that influence meaning since the realm of technology is an integral part of the world, it would therefore be expected that technology and its components and accessories also carry connotations that have been individually or socially constructed. For example, the sight of a USB connector, or the symbol or blue LED of a wireless Bluetooth connection, could have instant meaning when they are interpreted within the context of people's life styles and intended activities, and people could therefore be cued by these symbols to anticipate how particular artefacts may 'fit' (or not) into their lives. The case-studies have revealed some of these semiotics in the context of MP3 players. For example, the photographs in Study-1 and Study-2 acted as the symbols and triggers for re-living and recounting past experiences and also creating and anticipating new ones using a little detail on the photographs, or as a whole. These photographs were deliberately chosen to be ones that were used in the marketing campaigns of these products. Therefore, the photographs were perhaps showing the devices at their best, and according to the narrative intended by the marketer. This is seen as part of the narrative that users are exposed to, and it would be uncharacteristic, abnormal and out-of-context to provide 'sanitized' or laboratory-based images. The participants were part of the culture where these images were present, and the studies would therefore have been closer to a normal encounter with such images. Further study could be undertaken to find the effect of the fidelity, size and quality of the photographs on the way the participants may perceive them.

The appearance of an artifact is therefore very important to the way people experience it, where the visual aspect is part of a complex message that has roles for the designer, artifact and consumer, as well as the context as perceived by the user and environment as a whole. The product may be seen as the "transmitter of the message" (Crilly et al. 2004, p. 550), while the user is the 'receiver': "the visual appearance of products is a critical determinant of consumer response… Judgments are often made on the elegance, functionality and social significance of products based largely on visual information. These judgments relate to the perceived attributes of products" (Crilly et al. 2004, p. 547). As part of their "framework for consumer response to the visual domain" (2004, p. 569) of products, Crilly et al. suggest that the visual aspects of a product communicates many types of information, such as stereotypes, similar products, metaphors, character, conventions and clichés. Therefore, *visual interaction* occurs in the early window-shopping, or catalogue browsing period in consumption, and is very much part of the user experience and should not be marginalised due to the lack of physical interaction. Therefore, 'interaction' does occur at early stages of UX, and it is born in the communicative activity and constructions that are between the designer, society and user. Of course, as implied here, constructions (e.g. stereotypes) occur before the visual messages are passed in that particular moment. In other words, investigating these constructions, in the early part of the consumption process, is just as important as exploring the physical interactions that occur once the consumer starts to use the product. Therefore, in order to measure the judgment of user experience over time, pre-interaction stages should be part of the experimental protocol of user research or usability studies, as well as the whole temporal range, physical time or otherwise, for the same object type. In this way, the 'whole story' may be available for analysis in order to shed light on the 'life-world' of the user.

Study-2 has shown that there is something very important about the on-going anticipation and evaluation of experience, where each 'experience' seeds the anticipations for the next 'experience'. For example, during the pre-interaction phase, where the participants only saw the photographs, they were rating according to their 'first-impressions' which were seeded by their past relevant experiences. Subsequently, some of their ratings changed upon physical interactions. The second ratings were therefore measuring their current experience compared to their previous experience, and future experiences. Of course, the physical interaction became a new experience in its own right. These new experiences are therefore part of the learning process that seed the anticipations for the next events, and so on. As Kelly puts it "it is the learning which constitutes experience" (1955, p. 120). However, learning may also occur vicariously, by watching advertising media, which in this context become 'demonstrations'. In this case, advertisers may try to help a potential-user understand the product and form anticipations that minimise negative mismatch or disenchantment, and thereby enhance the probability of positive evaluations, once physical interaction takes place.

Therefore, in Study-2, the ratings of the photographs of the MP3 players pre-interaction, are essentially measuring anticipation for the next stage, which in this case happened to be the interaction stage. This anticipation is anchored in previous knowledge (inferred or 'real'), before the participants turned up for the study. McCarthy and Wright (2003) also point out anticipation in their sense-making framework and emphasised that "we never come to technology unprejudiced" (2003, p. 42). Therefore, recording the post-interaction ratings is essentially measuring the anticipations for the next time the participant will encounter other related technological artifacts in the future.

6.1.3 Evaluation and Anticipation

In Kelly's PCT, the notion of 'anticipation' is reflected in its basic postulate where "a person's processes are psychologically channelized by the way in which he anticipates events" (1955, p. 32). Kelly also emphasises the link to Dewey's philosophical stance: "Dewey…envisioned the universe as an on-going affair which had to be anticipated to be understood" (1955, p. 108). Anticipation is seen here as the notion of bringing some body of real or inferred knowledge to an upcoming event, with an idea of what is about to happen. In this case anticipation can be close to *pre-interaction*, in the sense that it is interaction, but not of the physical kind. However, anticipation is not a prediction (Butt 2008, p. 38), or reflective exercise, but explicitly means to "embrace the future rather than merely catalogue the past" (Kelly 1955, p. 240), where the implications of forthcoming events are understood at a personal level, with a personal investment in mind. It is similar to the difference between merely predicting a horse to win, or placing a bet with something of value at stake. Such anticipations ultimately lead to preferences and evaluations of some kind, whether cognitive (reflective) or affective. Study-2 showed clear evidence of evaluation occurring pre- and post-interaction. It would seem that participants were able to evaluate the visual stimuli of the MP3 player photographs, by using some visual cues, and connect them to what they anticipated in terms of a physical experience. Thereby creating meaning in their anticipation. So, a device is seen as convenient when visual or interactive experience gives the user a sense of what to expect in terms of effort in use, e.g. size, or ease of use, or any of the constructs they use to make sense of their experiences.

In regards to anticipation being an expression of how a person has understood the situation, the user may want to validate their ability to understand this particular event, or larger event. Kelly makes it clear that *validation* is related to the cycles of experience and the degree of commitment or involvement in the anticipation: "Our experience corollary infers from the fundamental postulate that a person's construction system varies as he successively construes the replication of events... If a person makes only vague commitments to the future he receives only vague validational experience. If his commitments are incidental and fragmentary, he experiences fragmentary validation only. If his commitments are based on far reaching interpretations of the situation, he may construe the outcome as having sweeping significance" (Kelly 1955, p. 110).

Therefore, if a user commits to an anticipation for a construct that is important and has high implications, and there is a mismatch once interaction takes place, between what the user anticipates and what they experience, then a negative affective response is likely to occur as a symptom of such a mismatch. Jordan (1999, p. 4) suggested that consumers experience such implications in the form of 'consumer hierarchy of needs', where *functionality* comes first, followed by *usability* and then *pleasure*. Study-3 and Study-4 data showed evidence of participants mixing functionality and compatibility with relationships, and the need to know that they could get secondary benefits through such mixing. Study-4 data may have provided further demonstrations of such hierarchies, where participants constructed brand as a signpost to convenience in terms of compatibility, as well as 'style' and 'ease of use'. Importantly the same brand also pointed to the lack of reliability, which is an *inconvenience*. This ultimately led to difficult choices. This raises a question of the validity of Jordan's proposal of a clear set of needs that are in a particular order for people in general. However, there may well be such a hierarchy, but is perhaps idiosyncratic, and is therefore in a different order for different people.

There were also several examples of anticipations in the data, with both positive and negative evaluations. These include the frustrations shown with one device, contrasting with the very positive reactions from other participants, for the same device. Although individual participants may have shown some consistency of preferences across devices, their opinions were shown to be liable to switch quickly, as well as demonstrate brand-resilience. For example, some participants were surprised by the ease of use of a particular device (suggesting a mismatch between actual and anticipated experience), yet other participants reported exactly the opposite experience. Such results demonstrated the difficulty and the merits of a 'one design for all' strategy. On the other hand, these effects may explain the successes that some manufacturers have enjoyed when they offer a wide range of models, in a range of colours and design skews that cater for the 'long-tail' of idiosyncratic preferences. Designers could take more advantage of this phenomenon by allowing mass customization of products to individual taste.

Of course, the above idiosyncratic or a general hierarchy of consumer needs, may be an oversimplification, and effects such as confirmation bias and emotions will also play a role in people changing their opinion. According to Kelly (1955), emotions may be seen as changes in the construct system, as Butt puts it: "disturbances in sense-making lead to a variety of states that we call emotional" (Butt 2008, p. 48). For example, *guilt*: "awareness of dislodgement of the self from one's core role structure", or *fear*: "awareness of imminent incidental change in one's core structure" (Kelly 1955, p. 391). McCoy (1981) has elaborated Kelly's view by addressing more emotions e.g. *love*: "awareness of validation of one's core structure", or *anger*: "awareness of invalidation of constructs leading to hostility" (McCoy 1981, p. 97). As McCoy makes clear, it is not the "outcome of the prediction" involved in the construct, but "its success or failure", i.e. whether the person feels that they are able to predict and anticipate the world 'correctly'. Such validation of the anticipation will result in positive or negative emotions. It is important to note that, just because there is validation on one level, does not mean there is validation on all levels. For example, a person could still feel an emotional response, even though they were 'right' in anticipating that their hard-disk is going to fail.

During the physical interaction in Study-2, participants often exhibited a positive affective evaluation when met with unexpected and pleasant aspects of the interface, as well as showing a neutral response (i.e. not commenting or not showing signs of a response to the stimulus) when they had a sense of progress towards their goal. Hsee and Abelson (1991) refer to this sense of progress as 'velocity'. However, when this velocity was negative, i.e. they sensed that they were not advancing or are being thwarted by the interface, or device, they showed a decidedly negative evaluative response. This is the kind of response that Jordan (1999) focuses on, which he refers to as the 'four pleasures', and ignores the finer grain of user experience. Norman (2003) on the other hand, proposes cognition to encompass reflective and interpretive processes, with emotion being portrayed as a "system for value judgement". Although the above views can be seen as different starting points, however, they are all pointing to the 'end point', or 'evaluation' of experience.

Therefore, even though the emotional thread maybe a useful 'idea' to hold as an important aspect of UX, as others have suggested (McCarthy and Wright 2004; Norman 2003), according to PCT, it is not a process that is separate to construction, but a symptom of the process of construction. Consequently, from a constructivist point of view, it may be misleading to place attention on emotion as something with causal power over experience. Nonetheless, although emotions are clearly relevant to how people experience technology, it is however a vast topic, and is not the focus of this book (see for example Boehner et al. 2007).

Even though emotion itself may not be of direct study, factors that influence it may be evident in the data within the case-studies. For example, the mismatch between anticipated and actual experience may be reflected in the absolute change in ratings (Z values), where a user may have an idea of what to expect and then react: "oh! I thought it was...but it turned out..." This indicates a mismatch between anticipated and actual perceived experience, which was also found by Swallow et al., where they concluded that their "data suggest that there may be a large gap between the expectations generated by marketing and the actual experiences in practice of representative users" (2005, p. 98). In this case, high Z values indicate high mismatch. In fact, the data in Study-2 showed that such events are likely to occur with a specific set of constructs that have been termed 'volatile' constructs, more so than with 'stable' constructs.

The most volatile constructs were for example: *unusual, pleasurable, not conventional*, and *not typical*. This suggests that photographs are likely to 'lie', and show devices as more 'interesting' than they may be upon close inspection after physical interaction. The most stable constructs, on the other hand, were for example: *understandable, not cluttered, functional* and *good brand identity*. This suggests that users are not likely to change their minds about aspects related to usability. It is interesting that good brand identity is the most stable of all constructs. This gives more credence to the idea that people are less likely to change their mind about the brand aspect of a device, based on one iteration or cycle of interaction. A possible avenue of further research is to explore links between volatility and meaningfulness. Hinkle (1965) suggested that more meaningful constructs, are ones that have the most *implications*. Therefore, it may be possible that anticipations with wider ranging implications may tend to influence preferences and ratings more.

This is not to say that stable constructs are not evaluative (e.g. leading to like or dislike decisions), it is just that the evaluation tends to be resilient to change post-interaction, whereas volatile constructs are more susceptible to change through use. Essentially, participants would have already had their anticipations with the photo-rating session, regarding the stable constructs, and the interaction did not give them a strong mismatch. Whereas, for volatile constructs, their anticipations brought to the photo-session were 'erroneous', and led to a subsequent feeling of mismatch during actual interaction. Such reconstruing could eventually lead to emotional evaluative responses, to *disenchantment*, or *enchantment* in the case of being pleasantly surprised (McCarthy et al. 2006; NíChonchúir and McCarthy 2008).

This idea of mismatch could also be applied to Tractinsky et al.'s study (2000), where participants were not entirely naïve because they had already encountered ATM interfaces in real life, and used them. They therefore had a notion of 'typical' layouts of ATM interfaces. This could mean that the study was not only measuring aesthetics and usability, but also measuring the responses due to discrepancy from typicality. This notion of discrepancy was described by Purcell (1986) in his *Schema Discrepancy Model*, where affect was attributed to a departure from what is typical or expected. In Study-2, however, the knowledge and anticipations that the participants brought to the study are considered part of their evolving user experience and evaluations. These anticipations were then exposed in the form of ratings. This knowledge that is brought to an event is modified upon subsequent visual (image) and physical interactions with the next, similar, or any other physical device. Importantly however, all previous knowledge being brought to an event, includes the 'lack-of-knowledge', i.e. what they do not know is part of their general anticipation. Therefore, volatility is an indication of a susceptibility to change, and is a dimension of a construct, with *volatile* and *stable* being the two poles of the dimension. Volatility is therefore related to the mismatch between anticipated and actual experiences, and the readiness to 'give up' an already made up mind.

However, it may be more useful to consider *stability* as the dimension (not volatility), where brand identity is one of the stable constructs (Study-2). Also, the data in Study-3 showed brand resilience, and may provide a window regarding the reasons for such stability. It seems that if the brand points to a construct, for example 'ease of use', and the same brand points to another construct, for example 'unreliable', then if 'ease of use' is higher on the order of hierarchy of importance or implications, then experience or evidence of 'unreliability' do not have enough 'power' to overturn the choice, or preference for the device. Therefore, it may be possible to consider such a concept as *Construct Power*, which is a product of the construct's hierarchy and stability:

$$\text{Construct Power} = \text{'Hierarchy Order'} \times \text{'Stability'}$$

The *Hierarchy Order* is unsigned (i.e. not a negative number), and has no valance in terms of 'good' is high, or 'bad' is low, but the higher the value the more important the construct. Therefore, if a construct has a high value for Hierarchy Order and a high value for Stability, then a direct negative experience is less likely to result in the user changing their stance on their evaluation, and are therefore likely to keep their opinion unchanged. However, if the construct has a low order in hierarchy, or a low stability value, then the evaluation is likely to change if a user finds evidence to contradict their previous opinion, and therefore change their mind.

Hassenzahl suggested that ratings and preferences were related to the type of construct, e.g. hedonic or pragmatic. In his study, using virtual interactive products, he showed that "pragmatic attributes as well as goodness were affected by experience (i.e. usability problems), whereas hedonic attributes and beauty remained stable over time" (2004b, p. 340). Hassenzahl refers to the increase in mental effort as a primary cause of the change in usability ratings (2004b, p. 339). Importantly, the real and physical aspects of interaction were missing from that study, and the data in Study-2 show that formal aesthetics (e.g. *Classic* and *Sleek*) and physicality (e.g. *Heavy* and *Bulky*) constructs are amongst the most volatile constructs, suggesting that mismatch can occur with both, 'pragmatic' as well as 'hedonic' aspects of interaction.

6.2 Dynamics

The third research question raised in this book was regarding the changes in UX as they occur throughout consumption and the phases within it, including the dynamics related to the constructs of UX as users move from intended to actualised consumption. Therefore, in trying to understand how evaluations and constructions change over time, first, the concept of *Time* with respect to UX, must be understood or at least defined. As discussed in Chap. 2, psychological time is a construction in its own right, and very different to real-time, which is measured on a clock. Psychological time is measured in meaning, and is inextricably linked to experience itself, as an unfolding and self-referencing phenomenon. Therefore, it is not possible to discuss constructions or evaluations in a static way. In other words, UX *must* be dynamic, which is why time is unavoidable, and is not a 'thread' that can be considered or not. However, Study-3 was designed to specifically explore the possibility of measuring experience in terms of consumption cycles, not physical time. For that, the CDP was used as a basis, and reduced to four basic meaningful phases in consumption (ABCD): *Approach*, *Buying*, *Consummation*, and *Dissolution*. These phases were also shown to be similar to Kelly's unit or quantum of experience.

The dynamics may be apparent in the form of the relationship between constructs. It may be possible that the change in the relationship between the superconstructs in the SSA plots in Study-2 (i.e. the move of the aesthetics group), hints towards a 'change in meaning' once interaction takes place, and in fact the 'relationship between the super-constructs' is a useful way to measure dynamics. Data in Study-2 showed evidence of such a way of differentiating types of experience, where the relationship between the constructs changed for different contexts. In that example, the individual constructs were in a particular configuration (visual interaction) in relation to each other (SSA plot), and then at a different type of experience (physical interaction), the relationship changed. This shows a constant state of flux for the relationship of the individual constructs, as well as the super-constructs. This raises some possibility for further research, where the relationship between the super-constructs in a long-term context may be explored.

6.3 Relationships

As discussed above, relationships are a key aspect of UX, and as shown in Chap. 2, Forlizzi and Ford (2000) proposed a model of experience that emphasised the relationship between the user and the object, as well the underlying context of use. In a later publication, Forlizzi and Battarbee (2004), focused their attention on the social interaction aspect of experience. Indeed, the case-study data presented here did show relationships of different types being evident as a dominant theme during the interviews, especially for Study-3. Therefore, relationships take on a central role where the *Self* is seen as central, and is related to different types of 'other': *Others*, *Brand* and *Object*. Although, McCarthy and Wright (2004) do make explicit reference to relationships being important to UX, aside from the above mentioned proposed models, only Battarbee and Mattelmäki (2002) make relationships a key aspect of their model, as discussed in Chap. 3. In contrast, social psychology studies often refer to such relationships (Csikszentmihalyi and Rochberg-Halton 1981; Dittmar 1992; Richins 1994; Wallendorf et al. 1988), and in the context of PCT,

Butt (2008) reiterates the prevalence of relationships and states that "our lives are made up of networks of relationships" (Butt 2008, p. 129).

6.3.1 Defining 'Self'

There were several types of relationships that were illustrated by the data, some were with friends and family, some were with other users, and some relationships were with the manufacturers and suppliers of technology. Each type of relationship offered different challenges for the user as well as different opportunities for the users to derive positive outcomes. However, whichever the type of relationship, it is possible to suggest that they served to help the user to understand their sense of 'self'. This sense of self does not exist in a vacuum, in other words it exists in the social and cultural landscape. Over several research projects, Dittmar (2008) showed consumers to be engaged in identity building and 'repair' through their engagement with consumer culture. Moreover, Dittmar also makes it clear that there is overwhelming evidence for the "extended self" in the literature that the self "stretches beyond the boundaries of the physical body to include material possessions" (2008, p. 48).

In trying to draw links between the personal and social construing, Kalekin-Fisherman (2003) points to Bourdieu's 'habitus', which is the "cluster of dispositions, attitudes, orientations, postures, habits and values conveyed to individuals by their cultural surround" (2003, p. 146). This is perhaps pointing to social determinism as a way for the individual to construct their identity. Additionally, Kelly (1932) suggested that there is "no such thing as an individual unless you have a group" (quoted in Kalekin-Fisherman 2003, p. 143). Thus, in order for a person to understand themselves, a person still needs 'other' to understand 'self'. In other words, for a person to understand themselves, there needs to be a reference point, and in this case it is a 'group'. This reference point acts in the same way that a construct is "a way in which some things are construed as being alike and yet different from others" (Kelly 1955, p. 74), i.e. a pole of a construct. Such contrast may also be related to the "distinctions" that Bourdieu (1984) mentions, where people make choices or behave in a particular way, as a device to define themselves and distinguish themselves from other groups.

In the case-study data presented earlier, such distinctions sometimes took on the form of a demonstration and rendering of political views and values through relationship with supplier, e.g. independence and supporting the underdog. For example, people might consider how they relate to the device, and its perceived user-group, and ultimately this helps them define who they are, and the narrative they see themselves living. Consequently, relationships and the way they intertwine with the technology make such narratives inseparable from the artifacts themselves, or a particular user group, along with their accepted values and shared meanings (Moscovici 1984).

This kind of symbiosis can also be seen in other ways. Bakhtin's (1993) idea of "dialogicality" is that a *thing* cannot exist in a 'monolog', but in a constant unfinalisable 'dialogue' with other *things*, that serves to relate them to each other. According to Butt

(2008), even ideas are social and cannot exist singularly: "you cannot have an 'individual' thought" (2008, p. 23). This sense of dialogue could again be seen as close to Kelly's definition of a construct having poles, where an idea is understood by knowing what it is different to, and similar to. In other words, it is not possible to understand hot, without knowing cold. Equally, it is not possible to understand a particular MP3 in one's hand, without knowing its place in the many narratives, even if it is the first time a user sees such a thing, they would still understand it relative to some *thing*. This dialogue of self and other is very much part of McCarthy and Wright's view of user experience (2004, p. 71), and is part of the holistic approach they adopt.

6.3.2 Brand as Proxy

The above relationships can also be with suppliers and manufacturers, as well as with objects. The participants in the case-studies provided clear evidence of how they very much paid attention to 'brand'. Not only was brand seen as an association to a narrative that was told in the marketing and advertising media (Du Gay et al. 1997), but also related to the narrative that was shared amongst friends and user-groups, where there is a "shared understanding among people that give the symbol reality" (Dittmar 2008, p. 34). Brand was also seen as a very resilient construct, that withstood dysfunction of the technology, anger towards the supplier and manufacturer (dissociated from the 'brand' itself), bad manufacturing quality, etc.

It seemed that the brand was the 'sign' to many meanings, including the promise of the brand of course. The notion of 'cue utilisation' could be at work (see Hansen 2005, p. 424), where a user simply perceives a few cues that help them towards a whole group of predefined meanings, choices, and implications, therefore the brand may be offering statistical redundancy, whereby only a few bits of information are mapped to a large amount of data. In other words, brand is a proxy to many concepts and canned meanings. For example, it could mean "problems with compatibility of file formats", "dependence on one supplier", "being cool", "ease of use", etc. It could also mean all of the above examples in a complex network of implications and prior experiences, and these experiences may not be of the same direction, i.e. they could be contradictory. Therefore, the brand could point to opposite valances of meaning. In this way, a brand could be a sign that triggers the tension of a love/hate polar response, where the user feels torn, and may then experience what Kelly calls "slot rattling" between the two poles of a construct (Winter et al. 2008, p. 90).

6.3.3 Loving Objects

Finally, the nature of the relationships between users and artifacts, pre- or post-acquisition, may influence experience significantly. The importance of relationships between users and artifacts or possessions have already been discussed earlier. A consumer may be attracted to an object because of some nostalgic attachment. Equally, an object may hold a purely utilitarian purpose that is part of a daily routine. However, such relationships may be compared to the notion of 'love' in its different forms. Based on the empirically-corroborated 'triangular theory of love' between people (Sternberg 1986), Shimp and Madden (1988) suggested that people may have the same pattern of relationships with products. They referred to them as the Consumer-Object Relationships (COR). They describe eight different relations that are combinations of three extremes: yearning/passion (*motivation*), liking/intimacy (*affect*), and decision/commitment (*cognition*). However, Prümper et al. (1992) proposed another way of categorising user types: *occasional users, frequent users, beginners, general users*, giving user-object relationships a temporal dimension.

Study-3 also showed examples of these relationships. There was ample evidence for relationship with *other*. The relationships that some participants had with others around them were either helping their experience become more positive, or hindering them. There were examples of relationships with: *Brand* (including manufacturers and suppliers), and *Others* (friends, family, peers). Participants spoke to people about their impending purchase, and also after they acquired their devices, as well as paying attention to anonymous online reviews. There were also several references to the relationship they had with the suppliers and manufacturers, and it became evident that these relationship formed an important part of their experiences with the device itself. In some of the cases, these relationships contributed to an overall negative experience, whereas for other participants, these relationships enhanced their positive experience.

Interestingly, no other research in the UX literature makes a consideration of relationship of users with *other* in the way that is proposed here, where the relationships show parallels to inter-personal relationships, regardless of technology. This point of view is important because it shows technology as an extension of society that people live, with no particularly special status.

6.4 User Experience Networks

An important aspect of relationships that was not discussed in the previous section is how an artifact may be related to other artifacts. Although this could be seen to be a direct part of *Convenience* (e.g. compatibility between devices), it is also possible to see such relationships as something other than convenience. For example, there were several examples of participants in Study-3, where they discussed the compatibility and connectivity to software packages that would be used to upload or play music, and which computer platform it would work on etc., e.g. iTunes software, was a point to consider when considering the anticipated experience with the MP3 player of choice. However, this was not just about the actual compatibility, but about the implications, and anticipations associated with such factors. Some participants hated iTunes, others loved it. Either way, it illustrated that users 'extend' their anticipations and constructs past the isolated artifact itself, and onto related artifacts, which shows that preferences are not made on isolated artifacts, but 'the whole story', as they perceive it. Therefore, when a user chooses to buy a certain device, they are also making an explicit or implicit choice about the related software, and hardware that is connected to the use of the device they chose. However, extending these examples to the context of *relationships*, highlights the relationship of these constructs with others such as brand, self, and aesthetics. This interconnectedness of super-constructs is a good illustration of how User Experience really is a holistic notion, and resists a reductive approach where these super-constructs are measured separately to find some Cartesian causal relationship. Therefore, as McCarthy and Wright (2004) said for their model, these super-constructs should only be used as placeholders or 'ideas' for practitioners and designers to focus their attention, and not as a way to isolate constructs, to the exclusion of other constructs, in order to make design changes that target specific constructs. In other words, a designer must always keep an eye on the whole story.

The above interconnectedness could be referred to as *Construct Networks*, in the same way that Butt proposes that "new events are approached with a network of personal constructs" (Butt 2008, p. 45). However, such networks may also be described as *User Experience Networks*. These networks of associations and implications are necessarily based on both public and private meanings and experiences. In this way the experience network becomes the infrastructure that people would use in order to navigate their way through their past and anticipated user experience. Hinkle (1965) proposed a 'theory of implication', to describe the changes in constructs as a function of the implications of the events encountered. Such implications may lay dormant, and tacit, and only come to the surface once provoked by choices or questions.

Although these UX Networks have not been explicitly highlighted by other research and models of the dynamics of UX, Study-1 gave a very clear window into such networks when participants sorted cards for combined, or 'compound' constructs e.g. "large and usable". This concept of interconnected constructs is similar to *semantic networks* outlined by Quillian (1968) (see Johnson-Laird 1988, p. 100), or *implication networks* where decisions are based. Hinkle (1965) discussed 'laddering' as an experimental technique to be used with constructs, to access implications that are held in the participant's mind, which provides a window to their reasoning, decision making and therefore preferences and evaluations. As Holbrook and Hirschman (1982) put it, "one's purchase decision is obviously only a small component in the constellation of events involved in the overall consumption experience" (1982, p. 137).

Although UX Networks are out of the scope of this book, and may be a subject of further research, it may be useful to briefly connect this concept to the sense of interconnected constructs and meaning, as discussed in Chap. 2. Rose (2006) illustrates the basic structure of meaning as fundamentally a network-like structure: "The meaning of [a] concept... is given by its relationships to ... other concepts. Moreover, all these concepts tie into one another and form a *holistic* entity—an entire semantic network" (Rose 2006, p. 9). According to Lakoff, this view is called *objectivist cognition*, where it defines meaning as the "relationship between symbols" (Lakoff 1988, p. 120). Lakoff reminds the reader that this meaning is not based in the "world as experienced" (Lakoff 1987, p. 216), but on anticipated experience. He maintains that such anticipations deal with individual phenomena, not categories of phenomena (i.e. abstract categorisations). This distinction seems very relevant to the change in categorisation that was witnessed in the data in Study-2, where aesthetics were categorised differently once real interaction occurred, rather than anticipated experience. Barwise and Perry (1984) define "ecological realism", a view that finds "meaning located in the interaction between living things and their environment" (1984, p. 10). Kelly (1955) not only described constructs as existing in some relationship to each other, as part of his *Organisation corollary*, he also proposed an organised ordinal structure that is susceptible to change: "Within a construction system there may be many levels of ordinal relationships, with some constructs subsuming others and those, in turn, subsuming still others. When one construct subsumes another its ordinal relationship may be termed *superordinal* and the ordinal relationship of the other becomes *subordinal*. Moreover, the ordinal relationship between the constructs may reverse itself from time to time." (Kelly 1955, p. 40). It seems that Kelly almost predicted the results of Study-2 where the ordinal relationship between the super-constructs changed, and the Aesthetics region merged with some of the other regions. Further, there has also been empirical evidence (yet unpublished by the author) to suggest a clear hierarchy of self-reported 'importance' amongst super-constructs. This gives a hint toward some kind of 'rationale' to decision making based on the super-constructs and the UX networks.

References

Anderson, C. (2004). The Long Tail. *Wired*. Retrieved 14/08/2006, from http://www.wired.com/wired/archive/12.10/tail.html.

Bakhtin, M. (1993). *Toward a philosophy of the act*. Austin: University of Texas Press.

Barwise, J., & Perry, J. (1984). *Situations and attitudes*. Cambridge: MIT Press.

Battarbee, K., & Mattelmäki, T. (2002). *Meaningful relationships with products. Paper presented at the Proceedings of the Design and Emotions Conference, Loughborough.*

Berlyne, D. E. (1974). *Studies in the new experimental aesthetics: Steps toward an objective psychology of aesthetic appreciation*. Washington D.C.: Halsted Press.

Boehner, K., DePaula, R., Dourish, P., & Sengers, P. (2007). How emotion is made and measured. *International Journal of Human-Computer Studies, 65*, 275–291.

Bourdieu, P. (1984). *Distinction: A social critique of the judgement of taste*. London: Routledge.

Butt, T. (2008). *George kelly: The psychology of personal constructs*. Basingstoke: Palgrave Macmillan.

Crilly, N., Moultrie, J., & Clarkson, P. J. (2004). Seeing things: Consumer response to the visual domain in product design. *Design Studies, 25*(6), 547–577.

Csikszentmihalyi, M., & Rochberg-Halton, E. (1981). *The meaning of things*. Cambridge: Cambridge University Press.

Dittmar, H. (1992). *The social psychology of material possessions: To have is to be*. New York: St. Martin's Press.

Dittmar, H. (2008). *Consumer culture, identity and well-being: The search for the 'Good Life' and the 'Body Perfect'*. Hove: Psychology Press.

Du Gay, P., Hall, S., & Janes, L. (1997). *Doing cultural studies: The story of the Sony walkman*. London: Sage.

Forlizzi, J., & Battarbee, K. (2004). *Understanding experience. Paper presented at the Proceedings of DIS 2004, New York*.

Forlizzi, J., & Ford, S. (2000). *The Building Blocks of Experience: An Early Framework for Interaction Designers. Paper presented at the The conference on Designing Interactive Systems: processes, practices, methods, and techniques, New York*.

Hansen, T. (2005). Perspectives on consumer decision making: An integrated approach. *Journal of Consumer Behaviour, 4*(6), 420–437.

Hinkle, D. N. (1965). *The Change of Personal Constructs from the Viewpoint of a Theory of Implications*. (Unpublished Ph.D. thesis), Ohio State University, Columbus.

Holbrook, M. B., & Hirschman, E. C. (1982). The experiential aspects of consumption: Consumer fantasies, feelings, and fun. *The Journal of Consumer Research, 9*(2), 132–140.

Hsee, C. K., & Abelson, R. P. (1991). The velocity relation: Satisfaction as a function of the first derivative of outcome over time. *Journal of Personality and Social Psychology, 60*(3), 341–347.

Huang, M.-H. (2003). Designing website attributes to induce experiential encounters. *Computers in Human Behavior, 19*, 425–442.

Johnson-Laird, P. N. (1988). How is meaning mentally represented? In U. Eco, M. Santambrogio, & P. Violi (Eds.), *Meaning and mental representations*. Indianapolis: Indiana University Press.

Jordan, P. W. (1999). *Designing pleasurable products: An introduction to the new human factors*. London: Taylor and Francis.

Kalekin-Fisherman, D. (2003). Social relations in the modern world. In F. Fransella (Ed.), *International handbook of personal construct psychology* (pp. 143–152). Chichester: Wiley.

Kelly, G. A. (1932). *Understanding psychology. Unpublished manuscript: Copy in Fransella PCP collection, Universtiy of Hertfordshire, UK*.

Kelly, G. A. (1955). *The Psychology of Personal Constructs, Volume One: Theory and Personality* (1991 ed. Vol. 1). London: Routledge.

Lang, J. (1988). Symbolic aesthetics in architecture: Toward a research agenda. In J. L. Nasar (Ed.), *Environmental aesthetics: Theory, research and applications* (pp. 11–26). Cambridge: Cambridge University Press.

Lakoff, G. (1987). *Women, Fire, and Dangerous Things*. Chicago: University of Chicago Press.

Lakoff, G. (1988). Cognitive Semantics. In U. Eco, M. Santambrogio & P. Violi (Eds.), *Meaning and Mental Representations*. Indianapolis: Indiana University Press.

Lavie, T., & Tractinsky, N. (2004). Assessing dimensions of perceived visual aesthetics of web sites. *International Journal of Human-Computer Studies, 60*, 269–298.

Marx, K. (1978). Capital, Vol. 1. In R. C. Tucker (Ed.), *The Marx-Engels Reader* (pp. 294–438). London: W. W. Norton.

McCarthy, J., & Wright, P. C. (2003). Technology as experience (special issue). *Special Issue of Interactions Magazine: More Funology, 11*, 42–43.

McCarthy, J., & Wright, P. C. (2004). *Technology as experience*. Cambridge: MIT Press.

McCarthy, J., Wright, P. C., Wallace, J., & Dearden, A. (2006). The experience of enchantment in human-computer interaction. *Personal and Ubiquitous Computing, 10*(6), 369–378.

McCoy, M. M. (1981). *Positive and negative emotion: a personal construct theory interpretation*. London: Paper presented at the personal construct psychology, recent advances in theory and practice.

Moscovici, S. (1984). The Phenomenon of Social Representations. In R. Farr, M. & S. Moscovici (Eds.), *Social Representations* (pp. 3–69). Cambridge: Cambridge University Press.

NíChonchúir, M., & McCarthy, J. (2008). The enchanting potential of technology: A dialogical case study of enchantment and the internet. *Personal and Ubiquitous Computing, 12*(5), 401–409.

Nohl, W. (1988). Open spaces in cities: In search of a new aesthetic. In J. L. Nasar (Ed.), *Environmental aesthetics: Theory, research and applications* (pp. 74–83). Cambridge: Cambridge University Press.

Norman, D. A. (2003). *Emotional design: Why we love (or hate) everyday things.* New York: Basic Books.

Prümper, J., Zapf, D., Brodbeck, F. C., & Frese, M. (1992). Some surprising differences between novice and expert errors in computerized office work. *Behaviour and Information Technology, 11*(6), 319–328.

Purcell, A. T. (1986). Environmental perception and affect: A schema discrepancy model. *Environment and Behavior, 18*(1), 3–30.

Quillian, M. R. (1968). Semantic Memory. In M. L. Minsky (Ed.), *Semantic information processing* (pp. 227–270). Cambridge: MIT Press.

Richins, M. L. (1994). Valuing things: The public and private meanings of possessions. *Journal of Consumer Research, 21*(3), 504–521.

Rose, D. (2006). *Consciousness: Philosophical, psychological and neural theories.* Oxford: Oxford University Press.

Shimp, T. A., & Madden, T. J. (1988). Consumer-object relations: A conceptual framework based analogously on Sternberg's triangular theory of love. *Advances in Consumer Research, 15*, 163–168.

Sternberg, R. J. (1986). A triangular theory of love. *Psychological Review, 93*(2), 119–135.

Tractinsky, N., Shoval-Katz, A., & Ikar, D. (2000). What is beautiful is usable. *Interacting with Computers, 13*, 127–145.

Wallendorf, M., Belk, R. W., & Heisley, D. (1988). Deep meaning in possessions: The paper. *Advances in Consumer Research, 15*, 528–530.

Wilson, M. (1996). The socialization of architectural preferences. *Journal of Environmental Psychology, 16*, 33–44.

Winter, D. A., Duncan, J., & Summerfield, E. (2008). Love hurts: Exploration of love validation and conflict. *Personal Construct Theory and Practice, 5*, 86–98.

Zipf, G. K. (1949). *Human behavior and the principle of least effort.* Reading: Addison-Wesley.

Chapter 7
Conclusions

Abstract In the light of the findings, the concluding chapter highlights the role of designers and how they may take advantage of the super-constructs identified in the studies, as well as paying attention to the idiosyncratic nature of experience. In particular, the importance of anticipation, and early visual 'interactions,' are emphasised. Subsequently, the design and methodological limitations of the studies (including the case-studies) are discussed along with suggestions for further research. Practical implications for research and design are also explored before returning finally to the main research questions concerning the nature and dynamics of user experience. A concise statement summarises the conclusions that may be drawn from the data and discussions within the book. Particularly noteworthy is the contrast which may be drawn between the reductive and holistic view of UX. The major contributions of this book to the theory and practice within the fields of HCI and user experience are also highlighted.

Keywords Human–computer interaction (HCI) • Mobile device usability • Personal Construct Theory (PCT) • Sense making • User experience (UX) • User experience dynamics • UX-scale • ICE model • Design

In simple terms, experience is related to the extent that a person sees and understands the world around them, and this is something that may be exposed by finding out what they pay attention to, how they make meaning of it, and how salient that meaning is, because not all meanings are equal. To extend this understanding to 'user' experience would then require this definition to be focused on people who 'use' technology. This would therefore necessitate 'interaction' with a machine. A narrow view of a machine would conjure the early understandings of usability and ergonomics. However, perhaps a more accurate view of a machine would also include the 'meaning' of the machine to that person. Such meaning is not some isolated personal meaning, nor is it only the shared public meaning amongst a cultural cohort, but a combination of the two. The strength of the mix between these two is something that a designer of an artifact cannot predict, and it is this lack of prediction that renders *user experience* to be out of the complete control of the designer. However, a designer may indeed try to adjust the super-constructs and lay channels for relationships, and try to influence the social meanings, and therefore be able to *promote for* experience.

From a designer's point of view, however, the case-studies have demonstrated the importance of individual experiences in their idiosyncratic forms, as well as the shared experiences. The value of individualised experiences has been increasingly present in consumer literature. For example, Addis and Holbrook (2001) emphasise the value of bespoke, and customised consumption for individuals, against mass 'experiential consumption'. However, although *too much* choice can lead to negative affective responses (Schwartz 2004), some successful products address the paradox by allowing limited customisation and choice.

7.1 Limitations and Further Research

The methods described in the case-studies paid particular attention to the construction of user experience. Also, the variety of methods have made some way towards ensuring that there is no systematic filtering of one or more aspects of UX, thereby increasing confidence in the internal and external validity of the data. This multimethod approach started with the first method, the Multiple Sorting Procedure, which was very much about the discovery of how the participants understood their experience of MP3 player photographs, with the view of understanding their anticipated experience of actual MP3 players. As was presented in previous studies (Stamps 1990), photographs have been shown to be valid simulations of experience, and moreover, the 'catalogue' or 'web browsing' experience *is part* of the experience of an user in their approach to technology, including exposure to marketing media as a whole. Interestingly, the card-sorting task provided a particular advantage. This method, performed with images of MP3 players, provides the participant a tailored framework for discussing aesthetic and other constructs, and a way of exposing the 'connections' within their UX Network, and thereby providing a window to the dialogicality and holistic nature of the participant's experience with these particular devices, and related experiences. In other words, when a participant highlights or discusses a construct, they could be essentially exposing *why* it is important to them, i.e. what the implications are, and therefore also exposing what is of 'value' to them.

Nonetheless, Study-1 made a clear demonstration of the usefulness of the *Multiple Sorting Procedure* as an useful tool in accessing people's constructs as they experience technology, in this case, specifically for mobile media devices. However, the MSP technique may be used for any kind of experience with technology, as the technique uses participants' ability to distinguish differences and similarities between idea, concepts and experiences. The implication here is that this technique could be used to explore experiences themselves, using cards as 'place holders' (for further discussions on card-sorting see Spencer 2009; Tullis and Albert 2008, p. 222).

Another question of validity could be raised regarding the rating scales study (Study-2), due to the participant only being given the task to play with the devices, rather than being given a structured task with a goal. Again this is quite a normal scenario that is part of the overall experience that users have. For example, an user may go into a shop 'just to look around', or find a friend using a device, and be curious to borrow it briefly to examine it, or play with it without an underlying goal. Of course this means that further work could be undertaken, to extend the research and to explore goal-oriented experiences.

The interviews could also be criticised due to the intervention of the researcher by asking questions. In other words, the participants' experience after the interview was changed due to the recalling of the past events, in the frame and context of the questions from the researcher. Bruner (1986) makes this point of self-referencing experience, and is seconded by McCarthy and Wright (2004), where "the expression of experience is inherently problematic and dialogical. Thinking about and talking about experience changes it … that experience in turn shapes our expression of it" (McCarthy and Wright 2004, p. 118). This is of course an important point to raise. However, it could be argued that the kind of questions that were asked were nothing extraordinary, and could have been asked by a friend, or raised by reading the text on a blog site. Therefore, this is not a 'problem', but is part of the holistic nature of UX, and is a normal part of users' experience with technology.

However, even with the deliberate variety of methods used, it is possible to suggest that some other super-constructs have been missed due to the methods being insensitive to these other dimensions of UX. For this reason, the work presented in this book is seen as a starting point towards building an empirically grounded theory of UX. Therefore, the expectation is that more work will be done to verify these findings and perhaps explore the model in more detail. Also, as has been made clear at the beginning of this book, MP3 players were used as an exemplar of technology, and specifically, mobile personal media technology. It would be useful to explore the degree of generalisation of the findings with respect to other types of technology, for example non-mobile devices such as TV, cars, toasters etc. Also, possible differences maybe found by exploring owned versus public or shared technology, for example a parking ticket machine, ATM, commercial aeroplane, hospital equipment etc. Importantly though, all the examples given above are real objects, and it maybe useful to examine virtual objects, such as web sites and software in general, or even services such as SMS, or 'cloud' applications, where the software application 'resides' in some virtual location that is not only remotely located away from the user, but is located in any number or combination of locations.

The idea of having a *UX-profile* for a technology-based event or artifact could be used to characterise the experiences, or artifacts, themselves. For this to occur, the UX-Scales (Appendix D) could be used to measure the constructs or super-constructs, which would give a 'fingerprint' of the artifact. Such a UX-profile could be used to report or monitor dynamics of UX. However, more work needs to be undertaken to find ways of 'measuring' the interconnectedness of experiences and relationships that are so important to UX.

Finally, an useful avenue of research might be towards the relationship networks in technology, i.e. the sociality of technology itself. In other words, how does technology and the artifacts that manifest it relate to each other to create the technology society? And how do people engage with that society? In other words, what is the nature of the interface between the human society and the technology society? And, perhaps other kinds of societies.

7.2 Implications for Research and Design

This book started by questioning the nature of user experience, and after a review the relevant literature, a new model (ICE) was proposed which placed *Construction* as a process at the centre of experience. This proposal was supported by Kelly's PCT, as well as *Interaction* being central to the notion of 'user' of technology. Also, in all of its guises, *Evaluation* seems to be core to how people experience technology. The rest of the research was devoted to anchoring this model in empirical evidence. This was done for a single technology-type: physical, interactive, digital, personal, media-player. For this type of technology, a wide-range of UX-dynamics have been explored; from visual-stimuli, through to use, eventually to dissolution. The ICE model adds to and corroborates some of the existing ideas and data in the current literature in many ways, and the results from this research have enhanced this model.

Overall, PCT was used as the starting point to make a model of UX, which has much in common with the approach that McCarthy and Wright (2004) took. They used pragmatic philosophy as their starting point, which gives the two approaches significant overlap. For example, they point out that *anticipation* is an important process in sense making, whereas in PCT, it is as central to sense making as constructs are. Also, PCT has a well-developed methodology behind it, including derivative methods such as MSP, which makes the approach in this project easy to implement from a practitioner's point of view. However, in a deliberate attempt to avoid systematic errors that may be caused by using the same method or type of methods, this project has employed a multi-methods strategy, which has contributed to the enrichment of the data with complimentary insights.

However, for this research project, there have been some very clear findings that contribute to the body of knowledge towards understanding UX, and specifically for mobile media devices. First, Study-1 yielded a list of 89 constructs and categories of how the participants conceptualised MP3 players at a first-impression from a photograph, as well as for the construct of 'kinds of beauty'. An important new finding, which was later found in Study-2, is the categorisation of constructs to some that are more *stable* than others, which may be seen as more *volatile*. These data were also used to identify exemplars of MP3 players, which showed commonality with dimensions of preference: *shape*, *colour*, *screen*, and *orientation*. These dimensions were also complimented with the finding of the main split in preference of *modern* and *post-modern* groups. However, a key new empirical finding that follows from the initial list of constructs, is the classification of these constructs into seven, dimensions (7D-UX), super-ordinate constructs, 'super-constructs', that show themes that participants use to make sense of their experience with MP3 players: *Novelty*, *Usability*, *Complexity*, *Aesthetics*, *Physicality*, *Convenience*, and *Value*.

An important contribution has been the empirical evidence, from Study-2, for the difference in conceptualisation between *anticipated interaction* and *physical interaction*. This finding has shown the way that aesthetics are evaluated in such a way that they are interleaved with interaction, where physical interaction was shown as a way of going around the cycle of experience, that is different from experience that is *reflected* and anchored in past experiences only. Therefore, constructs of technology make different sense upon interaction, where anticipation and intention play out. Therefore, although aesthetics may be involved in usability, and as previous studies have shown a distinction between actual and perceived usability, there seems to be a distinction between *interactional* and *perceived* aesthetics. Therefore, designers should pay particular attention to users' anticipations as a key theme, coupled with context, and intentions: "Our expectations—and therefore our perceptions—are biased by three factors: the past: our experience, the present: the current context, and the future: our goals" (Johnson 2010, p. 1).

Although not reproduced or discussed in this book, a central contribution from Study-2 data was a UX-Scale that allows the measurement of the first five super-constructs: *Novelty*, *Usability*, *Complexity*, *Aesthetics*, and *Physicality*. This scale reported very high Cronbach's Alpha reliability scores, and could be used by other researchers to measure people's experience for these super-constructs.

One of the prominent themes to appear from the case-studies was 'relationships'. This theme came across in a variety of ways. However, as already mentioned, the data was reported with a focus on relationships between the *Self*, and *other* (social, brand, and object), as well as relating to other experiences. These findings gave more credence and support towards the hypothesis that UX is a holistic entity, and that a reductive description in other studies may be too naïve. This network of relationships was also evident from the dynamic relationship between constructs (Study-2), which gave a good demonstration of the interconnections and implications of UX-Networks. Since the very nature of meaning is about how one entity is related to another (discussed in Chap. 2), and as Osgood et al. (1957) define it, meaning is about "relating signs to their significates" (Osgood et al. 1957, p. 3), it follows that relationships are key to meaning. Since, meaning is central to experience, it follows that relationships are therefore key to experience. Importantly, these relationships can have a momentary nature (e.g. can be felt or described in mid conversation while relaying a story or experience), as well as on-going, and more of a steady nature, which may be shared with others. Thereby emphasising the phenomenological aspect of experience, where accessing people's ways of relating to others, and to their own other experiences is an important part of any method or tool that may be used in the study of UX.

By way of an analogy, music is perhaps useful in trying to relay the idea of UX being a holistic psychological event. Music is felt very differently when heard as individual notes or phrases, rather than as a whole melody. However, it is important to be reminded of the difference to the quality of the music if the same notes are played on distorted guitar, bassoon, violoncello, or Arabian oud. Such an analogy raises questions about the 'quantum' of music, and if indeed it is a 'note'. In this case, the question moves from the realm of music to the study of sound. Smaller parts of a note can now be discussed in a meaningful way, where duration and quality can be described using a different notation and nomenclature (e.g. milliseconds, frequency). Therefore, in Kelly's (1955) terms; it depends on the 'range of convenience', i.e. no theory or construct is 'fit-for-purpose' for all situations or contexts. It depends.

Kelly also explains construction as the act of relating one event to another, and this is 'construing'. Therefore, 'relationships' do not hold some special place in the ICE model, but are simply 'constructions'. This would therefore suggest that ICE may be sufficient as a model describing the interconnected basic processes of UX, and is perhaps useful for understanding UX, along with the seven basic super-constructs. Therefore, to return to the basic question about the nature of User Experience, the empirically derived, full version of the ICE model now suggests a plausible answer to this questions, having being enhanced with finer details (Fig. 7.1). Some elements are seemingly reductive, and some elements emphasise the holistic view, however, the model should be viewed while keeping *self* and interconnected and ubiquitous *relationships*, in their different guises, in the foreground.

However, just as McCarthy and Wright (2004) have used specific processes, or as they call them "ideas", that are helpful when thinking about UX, the ICE model also offers a designer some well defined aspects that maybe attended to that are less abstract than the processes illustrated by McCarthy and Wright. For example, the super-constructs suggest to the designer that *novelty*, or *complexity* are dimensions of UX that they can develop and work with, and still, these should not be treated as isolated levers. A designer may therefore apply the ICE model and the super-constructs, and the focus on self and relationship to enhance pre-existing design methods such as the one developed by Doblin to design a compelling user experience (See Kumar 2013, p. 178). In this example, a designer could explore ways of enhancing each of the super constructs in the context of the phases of experience described by the Doblin method, which already has many parallels with the Consumer Decision Process (CDP), described in Chap. 5.

Fig. 7.1 A schematic representation of the seven super-constructs found in the case-studies, as well as the central position that self and relationships hold within a holistic user experience

Finally, to return to the question raised at the start of this book regarding the reaction of the individuals at the iPhone launch, it is possible to suggest that the iPhone, was in its own right, an expectation and an anticipation. It would be naïve to suggest that the response was entirely due to what they saw at that moment. The response was also due to the well-orchestrated and constructed narrative and 'show' by a deliberate marketing campaign. In that way, the people in the auditorium had started their interaction with it long before the launch event, and the specific marketing campaign. Importantly, there was no particular 'point' where the interaction started, physical or otherwise. Such interactions are diffuse and do not have delineated start or finish lines. People's general day-to-day living, that connects them with the myriad of technologies and hearing others recounting their experiences, is where interactions and perceptions are shaped. The point where people finally get to use the technological artifacts is just another point of contact that will ultimately influence future interactions with the next generation of phones that will follow that iPhone, such as the more 'democratic' and open-source based Android phones, where other social forces are involved. In fact, as this research was being finalised, there was more evidence of the perpetual 'experience mill' that promotes anticipations within well orchestrated narratives, where the BBC's anticipatory headline read "Apple to unveil new product, amid swirl of speculation" (Shiels 2010), which was then followed by Wired Magazine, reporting that "[Apple] launched one of the most anticipated products in years" (Lanxon and Scott 2010), and Reuters agreed that it "rivals the smartphone [iPhone] as the most anticipated in Apple's history" (Madway and Oreskovic 2010). It was of course, the iPad.

In the mean time, maybe the balance of power is slowly shifting. Currently, 3D printers are quickly coming of age, and are already available at low cost, where it is possible for someone to make their devices in customised form-factors, from a choice of materials, and freely available production plans. Such trends may serve to challenge traditional HCI practitioners towards rethinking ways of running research studies, where customised products become more prevalent. This phenomenon may nudge ICE further towards the user's control, where these devices may one day allow average users and consumers to define the attributes of their *super-constructs*, to better fit their preferred ways of *interaction*, in order to have a more predictable *evaluation*, promoting more personalised, and perhaps optimal, user experience.

References

Addis, M., & Holbrook, M. B. (2001). On the conceptual link between mass customisation and experiential consumption: An explosion of subjectivity. *Journal of Consumer Behaviour, 1*(1), 50–66.

Bruner, E. M. (1986). Introduction: Experience and its expression. In V. Turner & E. M. Bruner (Eds.), *The anthropology of experience*. Illinois: University of Illinois Press.

Johnson, J. (2010). *Designing with the mind in mind: Simple guide to understanding user interface design rules*. Burlington: Morgan Kaufmann.

Kelly, G. A. (1955). *The psychology of personal constructs, vol. 1: Theory and personality* (1991 ed. vol. 1). London: Routledge.

Kumar, V. (2013). *101 design methods: A structured approach for driving innovation in your organisation*. Hoboken: Wiley.

Lanxon, N., & Scott, K. (2010). *Apple unveils its 'tablet'—The Apple iPad*, Retrieved 27/01/2010, from http://www.wired.co.uk/news/archive/2010-01/27/apple-unveils-its-%27tablet%27—the-ipad.aspx.

Madway, G., & Oreskovic, A. (2010). *Apple unveils $499 iPad, bets on new device class*, Retrieved 27/01/2010, from http://uk.reuters.com/article/idUKN2720449120100127.

McCarthy, J., & Wright, P. C. (2004). *Technology as experience*. Cambridge: MIT Press.

Osgood, C. E., Suci, G. J., & Tannenbaum, P. H. (1957). *The measurement of meaning*. Urbana: Illinois University Press.

Schwartz, B. (2004). *The paradox of choice: Why more is less*. New York: Harper Collins.

Shiels, M. (2010). *Apple to unveil new product, amid swirl of speculation*, Retrieved 26/01/2010, from http://news.bbc.co.uk/1/hi/technology/8480063.stm.

Spencer, D. (2009). *Card sorting: Designing usable categories Brooklyn*. New York: Rosenfeld Media.

Stamps, A. E. (1990). Use of photographs to simulate environments: A meta-analysis. *Perceptual and Motor Skills, 71*, 907–913.

Tullis, T., & Albert, B. (2008). *Measuring the user experience: Collecting, analyzing, and presenting usability metrics*. Burlington: Morgan Kaufman.

Appendix A
Photographs of MP3
Players Used in Eliciting Constructs

Case-Study 1
(Reproduced with permission from Al-Azzawi et al. 2007. Taylor & Francis Ltd.
www.tandfonline.com)

A. al-Azzawi, *Experience with Technology*, SpringerBriefs in Computer Science,
DOI: 10.1007/978-1-4471-5397-9, © The Author(s) 2014

Reprinted with permission from Taylor & Francis

Appendix B
Sample of Rating-Sheet
for Pre- and Post-interaction Study

Case-Study 2

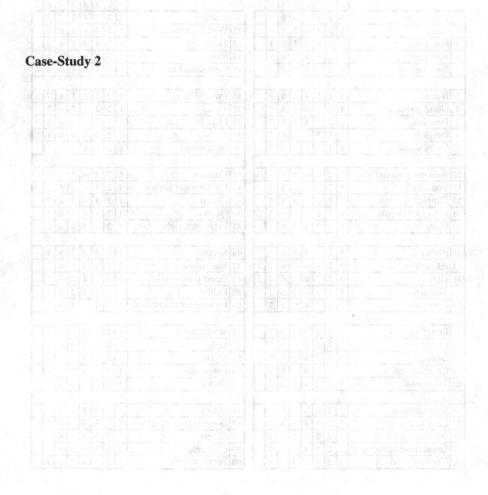

A. al-Azzawi, *Experience with Technology*, SpringerBriefs in Computer Science,
DOI: 10.1007/978-1-4471-5397-9, © The Author(s) 2014

| Participant No. | B- | | MP3 Player | 1 | 2 | 3 | 4 | | Part: | 1 | 2 |

Please rate **the extent to which you think each description applies to the MP3 player**. If you feel that you do not have enough information to make a judgement, make your best guess on the basis of what you see, and tick the box "*Not Enough Information*".

		Strongly Disagree	Disagree	Somewhat disagree	Neither agree nor disagree	Somewhat agree	Agree	Strongly agree	Not Enough Information
1	Expensive	1	2	3	4	5	6	7	
2	Heavy	1	2	3	4	5	6	7	
3	Feminine	1	2	3	4	5	6	7	
4	Average	1	2	3	4	5	6	7	
5	Nice colour	1	2	3	4	5	6	7	
6	Beautiful	1	2	3	4	5	6	7	
7	Good screen size	1	2	3	4	5	6	7	
8	Practical	1	2	3	4	5	6	7	
9	Original	1	2	3	4	5	6	7	
10	Good shape	1	2	3	4	5	6	7	
11	Well designed controls	1	2	3	4	5	6	7	
12	Too small	1	2	3	4	5	6	7	
13	Simple	1	2	3	4	5	6	7	
14	For older people	1	2	3	4	5	6	7	
15	Cute	1	2	3	4	5	6	7	
16	Pleasing	1	2	3	4	5	6	7	
17	Attractive	1	2	3	4	5	6	7	
18	Dull	1	2	3	4	5	6	7	
19	Technological	1	2	3	4	5	6	7	
20	Compact	1	2	3	4	5	6	7	
21	Functional	1	2	3	4	5	6	7	
22	Classic	1	2	3	4	5	6	7	
23	Boring	1	2	3	4	5	6	7	
24	Complicated	1	2	3	4	5	6	7	
25	Trustworthy	1	2	3	4	5	6	7	
26	Eye-catching	1	2	3	4	5	6	7	
27	Easy to use	1	2	3	4	5	6	7	
28	Well designed	1	2	3	4	5	6	7	
29	Good specifications	1	2	3	4	5	6	7	
30	Conventional	1	2	3	4	5	6	7	

		Strongly Disagree	Disagree	Somewhat disagree	Neither agree nor disagree	Somewhat agree	Agree	Strongly agree	Not Enough Information
31	Sleek	1	2	3	4	5	6	7	
32	Well Constructed	1	2	3	4	5	6	7	
33	Too large	1	2	3	4	5	6	7	
34	Shiny	1	2	3	4	5	6	7	
35	Convenient to use	1	2	3	4	5	6	7	
36	I would buy	1	2	3	4	5	6	7	
37	Tacky	1	2	3	4	5	6	7	
38	I like it	1	2	3	4	5	6	7	
39	Trendy	1	2	3	4	5	6	7	
40	Nice shape	1	2	3	4	5	6	7	
41	Unusual	1	2	3	4	5	6	7	
42	For younger people	1	2	3	4	5	6	7	
43	Cheap	1	2	3	4	5	6	7	
44	Quirky	1	2	3	4	5	6	7	
45	Light in weight	1	2	3	4	5	6	7	
46	Sporty	1	2	3	4	5	6	7	
47	Masculine	1	2	3	4	5	6	7	
48	Good functionality	1	2	3	4	5	6	7	
49	Fiddly	1	2	3	4	5	6	7	
50	I would recommend it	1	2	3	4	5	6	7	
51	Streamlined	1	2	3	4	5	6	7	
52	Ugly	1	2	3	4	5	6	7	
53	Stylish	1	2	3	4	5	6	7	
54	Futuristic	1	2	3	4	5	6	7	
55	Bulky	1	2	3	4	5	6	7	
56	Dinky	1	2	3	4	5	6	7	
57	Good brand identity	1	2	3	4	5	6	7	
58	Elegant	1	2	3	4	5	6	7	
59	Cluttered	1	2	3	4	5	6	7	
60	Feels smooth	1	2	3	4	5	6	7	

| Participant No. | B- | MP3 Player | 1 2 3 4 | Part: | 1 2 |

Please rate **the extent to which you think each description applies to the MP3 player**. If you feel that you do not have enough information to make a judgement, make your best guess on the basis of what you see, and tick the box "*Not Enough Information*".

		Strongly Disagree	Disagree	Somewhat disagree	Neither agree nor disagree	Somewhat agree	Agree	Strongly agree	Not Enough Information			Strongly Disagree	Disagree	Somewhat disagree	Neither agree nor disagree	Somewhat agree	Agree	Strongly agree	Not Enough Information
61	Mysterious	1	2	3	4	5	6	7		91		1	2	3	4	5	6	7	
62	Understandable	1	2	3	4	5	6	7		92		1	2	3	4	5	6	7	
63	Exciting	1	2	3	4	5	6	7		93		1	2	3	4	5	6	7	
64	I need this device	1	2	3	4	5	6	7		94		1	2	3	4	5	6	7	
65	It will do the job	1	2	3	4	5	6	7		95		1	2	3	4	5	6	7	
66	Useful	1	2	3	4	5	6	7		96		1	2	3	4	5	6	7	
67	Typical	1	2	3	4	5	6	7		97		1	2	3	4	5	6	7	
68	Complex (visually)	1	2	3	4	5	6	7		98		1	2	3	4	5	6	7	
69	Novel	1	2	3	4	5	6	7		99		1	2	3	4	5	6	7	
70	Easy to control	1	2	3	4	5	6	7		100		1	2	3	4	5	6	7	
71	Usable	1	2	3	4	5	6	7		101		1	2	3	4	5	6	7	
72	Can access its functionlity easily	1	2	3	4	5	6	7		102		1	2	3	4	5	6	7	
73	Reminds me of something else	1	2	3	4	5	6	7		103		1	2	3	4	5	6	7	
74	I can understand it	1	2	3	4	5	6	7		104		1	2	3	4	5	6	7	
75	Complex (functionality)	1	2	3	4	5	6	7		105		1	2	3	4	5	6	7	
76	It all fits together well	1	2	3	4	5	6	7		106		1	2	3	4	5	6	7	
77	I can find my way around it	1	2	3	4	5	6	7		107		1	2	3	4	5	6	7	
78	Lots to explore	1	2	3	4	5	6	7		108		1	2	3	4	5	6	7	
79	I am curious about it	1	2	3	4	5	6	7		109		1	2	3	4	5	6	7	
80	It is curious	1	2	3	4	5	6	7		110		1	2	3	4	5	6	7	
81	I connect it with my sense of self	1	2	3	4	5	6	7		111		1	2	3	4	5	6	7	
82	Strange	1	2	3	4	5	6	7		112		1	2	3	4	5	6	7	
83	Interesting	1	2	3	4	5	6	7		113		1	2	3	4	5	6	7	
84	Desirable	1	2	3	4	5	6	7		114		1	2	3	4	5	6	7	
85	It feels good to touch	1	2	3	4	5	6	7		115		1	2	3	4	5	6	7	
86	It feels good to hold	1	2	3	4	5	6	7		116		1	2	3	4	5	6	7	
87	It feels good to carry	1	2	3	4	5	6	7		117		1	2	3	4	5	6	7	
88	Pleasurable	1	2	3	4	5	6	7		118		1	2	3	4	5	6	7	
89	Nothing special	1	2	3	4	5	6	7		119		1	2	3	4	5	6	7	
90		1	2	3	4	5	6	7		120		1	2	3	4	5	6	7	

Appendix C
Interview Schedule: Long-term Dynamics of Experience

Case-Study 3 and 4

A. al-Azzawi, *Experience with Technology*, SpringerBriefs in Computer Science, 139
DOI: 10.1007/978-1-4471-5397-9, © The Author(s) 2014

(a) First interview

Dissolution and Divestment
1.   What did you think of the previous model?
2.   How does it compare to alternative models?
3.   What are you going to do with your previous model?

Approach

4. Why do you think you need an MP3 player?
5. Have you got any criteria (functionalities and attributes) for your choice?
6. Are there important issues to look out for?
7. Have you discussed your thoughts with anyone?
8. Have you started looking around yet?
9. When do you think you'll get it?
10. Who is going to pay for it?
11. What are you going to do next?

(b) Second interview

Buying (Acquisition)

12. How did you get on with your search?
13. What where the factors that influenced your final decision?
14. Where did you find the most useful information that helped you choose?
15. How was the purchasing experience?
16. What do you think about your choice?

(c) Third interview

Consummation (Use)

17. How are you getting on with your MP3 player?
18. Have your anticipations been fulfilled?
19. Have you been pleasantly or unpleasantly surprised by anything?
20. Are there any design recommendations you can make?
21. Would you recommend this product?

(d). Extra interviews

For some participants, extra interviews were held, and were essentially repeats of
the third interview.

Appendix D
UX-Scale

UX-Scale derived from data in Case-Study 2.

A. al-Azzawi, *Experience with Technology*, SpringerBriefs in Computer Science, 141
DOI: 10.1007/978-1-4471-5397-9, © The Author(s) 2014

Novelty	*Aesthetics*
Not dull	Cute
Trendy	Not dull
Technological	Trendy
Not boring	Technological
Not average looking	Streamlined
Looks special	Nice shape
Futuristic	Feels good to hold
Stylish	Pleasurable
Novel	Good brand
Desirable	Nice colour
Curious	Feels smooth
	Beautiful
Usability	Not ugly
Well designed	Unusual
Well constructed	Futuristic
Understandable	Good shape
Pleasurable	Stylish
Well designed controls	Quirky
Not cluttered	Feels good to carry
Beautiful	Novel
Usable	Attractive
Not ugly	Desirable
Convenient to use	Mysterious
Useful	Sleek
Easy to control	Elegant
Attractive	
Practical	
Can access its functionality	*Physicality*
Easy to use	Compact
Elegant	Cute
Functional	Light in weight
	Streamlined
Complexity	Not heavy
Complex (visually)	Nice shape
Not simple	Feels good to hold
Strange	Good brand
Complicated	Nice colour
Not conventional	Not too large
Complex (functionally)	Sporty
Unusual	Feels smooth
Quirky	Good shape
For younger people	Not bulky
Mysterious	Feels good to carry
Looks masculine	Sleek